CRYSTAL CLARITY

UNVEILING THE POWER OF GEMSTONES

DR. MINAKSHI BANSAL

DEDICATION

For all those who seek to uncover the hidden magic within themselves and the world around them.

❥❥❥

Contents

Contents

Contents

Prayer

"Om Bhadram Karnebhih Shrinuyama Devah

Bhadram Pashyemakshabhiryajatrah

Sthirairangais Tushtuvamsastanubhih

Vyashema Devahitam Yadayuh

Svasti Na Indro Vriddhashravah

Svasti Nah Pusha Vishwavedah

Svasti Nastarkshyo Arishtanemih

Svasti No Brihaspatir Dadhatu

Om Shantih Shantih Shantih"

This mantra is a prayer for universal well-being, invoking the blessings of various deities for protection, health, and happiness. It emphasizes the importance of experiencing the auspicious through all senses and living a life aligned with divine purpose. The repetition of "Shantih" at the end signifies a deep desire for peace in the individual, the environment, and the universe at large. This mantra is often recited as a prayer for peace, prosperity, and the physical and spiritual well-being of all beings.

༄༄༄

About The Author

This book represents the culmination of extensive research and meticulous analysis, incorporating a diverse range of sources, including numerous books, scholarly studies, and personal experiences. Additionally, I have scoured various websites to gather relevant information and data essential for the compilation of this work. I have taken every precaution to ensure the accuracy of the information presented and have diligently cited all sources to acknowledge their contributions.

From her earliest days, Minakshi was distinguished by an insatiable appetite for reading. Her literary universe was inhabited by characters and narratives that spanned ethical tales, motivational and inspirational stories, and the mythic parables imbued with life lessons. This voracious reading habit was not merely for personal edification but was driven by a desire to distill and disseminate the essence of these narratives to foster the development of students and peers alike. She was particularly captivated by the lives and teachings of historical figures and spiritual leaders such as Adi Shankaracharya, Swami Vivekananda, Dr. APJ Abdul Kalam, Mahamana Pandit Madan Mohan Malviya, Mahatma Gandhi, Sardar Vallabhai Patel, and Vinoba Bhave, among others. Their philosophies and life stories fueled her ambition to embody their ideals of resilience, selflessness, and relentless pursuit of knowledge.

Dr. Minakshi's academic and practical engagement with psychology has been equally noteworthy. As a research scholar, her focus has been on exploring the intricate tapestry of the human psyche, aiming to unlock the potential for psychological well-being and societal harmony. Her scholarly work is complemented by her active involvement in social work, where she employs her academic insights to make tangible differences in the lives of the underprivileged. Her endeavours in social work are characterized by an innovative approach that combines traditional wisdom with contemporary psychological practices to address the multifaceted challenges faced by these communities.

Her artistic talents, another facet of her diverse capabilities, are not merely a personal passion but also serve as a medium through which she communicates and connects with others. Her art, rich in symbolism and emotional depth, reflects her philosophical inquiries and social concerns, offering viewers a glimpse into the breadth of her intellect and the depth of her compassion.

In addition to her contributions to the arts and social sciences, Dr. Minakshi has embraced the healing arts of Pranic Healing, mastering the techniques developed by Master Choa Kok Sui. This practice, which focuses on the manipulation of Prana or life energy to heal the body and aura, has been both a personal journey of discovery and a means through which she extends her healing touch to others. Her proficiency in Pranic Healing is complemented by her advocacy and teaching of various forms of meditation aimed at rejuvenation, personal betterment, and the cultivation of harmony within individuals and communities alike.

Dr. Minakshi's life is a narrative of relentless pursuit, not just of personal achievement but of the upliftment and empowerment of society at large. Her diverse interests and talents—spanning the arts, literature, psychology, and the healing practices—converge on a singular path of service. She embodies the spirit of the luminaries who inspired her, channelling their legacy through her actions and teachings. Through her books, art, and social initiatives, she continues to inspire a new generation to embark on their own journeys of self-discovery, resilience, and altruism.

Her commitment to social betterment, particularly her focus on uplifting underprivileged children, reflects a deep understanding of the transformative potential of education and personal development. By integrating her knowledge of psychology, her artistic sensibilities, and her healing practices, Dr. Bansal has developed a holistic approach to social work that addresses both the immediate needs and the long-term well-being of the communities she serves.

As an author, Dr. Minakshi's writings offer a blend of inspirational insights, practical wisdom, and reflective contemplations drawn from her extensive reading and life experiences. Her books serve as a guide for those seeking to navigate the complexities of life with grace, resilience, and purpose. Through her narratives, she extends an invitation to her readers to explore the depths of their own potential and to contribute meaningfully to the collective well-being of society.

In Dr. Minakshi Bansal, we find a remarkable synthesis of the artist, the scholar, the healer, and the social activist. Her life's work stands as a beacon of hope and a source of inspiration for individuals seeking to make a difference in the world. Her story is a compelling reminder of the power of individual action, rooted in compassion and driven by a profound commitment to the betterment of humanity. Dr. Minakshi's legacy is not just in the tangible outcomes of her efforts but in the enduring spirit of inquiry, empathy, and service that she embodies.

ᐅᐅᐅ

Preface

In a world brimming with technology and a ceaseless hum of information, there exists a realm of quiet wisdom and profound healing – the realm of crystals. It is a world that has fascinated me since childhood, when I would pore over my grandmother's collection of sparkling stones, each one whispering stories of ancient civilizations, hidden magic, and the interconnectedness of all things.

In this book, I invite you to join me on a journey through this enchanting realm, where we will delve into the captivating beauty and powerful metaphysical properties of gemstones. We will explore their rich history, cultural significance, and the profound ways they can enhance our well-being, ignite our creativity, and connect us to our inner wisdom.

The study of crystals is not merely a scientific pursuit, but a spiritual one. It is a journey of self-discovery, where we learn to listen to the whispers of the Earth, connect with our intuition, and tap into the universal energies that flow through all of us. In this book, we will explore the concept of crystal healing, a holistic practice that utilizes the unique vibrations of gemstones to promote physical, emotional, and spiritual well-being. We will delve into the chakra system, the seven energy centers that govern our physical and emotional health, and discover how crystals can help to balance and align these centers, restoring harmony and vitality to our lives.

Each gemstone we encounter in this book has a unique story to tell. We will uncover the ancient myths and legends that have surrounded them for centuries, exploring their symbolism and cultural significance. We will also delve into their scientific properties, examining their chemical composition, crystal structure, and the fascinating ways they interact with light and energy. But most importantly, we will explore their metaphysical properties, the subtle energies that they emit and how they can impact our lives.

In this book, you will find a comprehensive guide to some of the most popular and powerful gemstones. We will explore the calming serenity of Amethyst, the unconditional love of Rose Quartz, the transformative power of Obsidian, and the radiant joy of Citrine. We will delve into the protective energy of Turquoise, the grounding strength of Tiger's Eye, the wisdom of Lapis Lazuli, and the passionate fire of Ruby. Each gemstone will be presented with its unique properties, historical significance, and practical applications for healing and personal growth.

Throughout this book, I will share my personal experiences and insights gleaned from years of working with crystals. I will offer practical tips and techniques for incorporating crystals into your daily life, from choosing the right stones for your specific needs to cleansing and charging them to maximize their effectiveness. I will also share meditations, rituals, and other practices that can help you to connect with the energy of crystals and harness their transformative power.

As you embark on this journey with me, I encourage you to approach the world of crystals with an open mind and a curious heart. Let go of any preconceived notions and allow yourself to be guided by your intuition. Remember, the most important factor in working with crystals is your intention and your connection to their energy. Trust your instincts, listen to your heart, and allow the wisdom of crystals to unfold in your life.

It is my hope that this book will serve as a guide and inspiration for your own crystal journey. Whether you are a seasoned crystal enthusiast or new to the world of gemstones, may you find within these pages the knowledge, inspiration, and practical tools you need to harness the power of crystals for healing, transformation, and personal growth. May the shimmering beauty and profound wisdom of crystals illuminate your path, and may their gentle energy guide you towards a life filled with joy, peace, and spiritual fulfillment.

Dr. Minakshi Bansal
Social Activist
Ahmedabad, Gujarat, Bharat

❧❧❧

ONE

AMETHYST: INNER PEACE AND INTUITION. SUBTITLE: THE STONE OF SERENITY.

Amethyst, a mesmerizing gem with its enchanting violet hues, has captivated humanity for millennia. Often dubbed "the stone of serenity," amethyst's allure extends beyond its visual appeal. It's a crystal steeped in rich history, lore, and metaphysical properties that resonate with the deepest parts of our being. Let's delve into the world of amethyst and explore the profound ways it can cultivate inner peace and intuition.

Amethyst's name originates from the ancient Greek word "amethystos," meaning "not intoxicated." The Greeks believed that amethyst could protect against drunkenness and maintain a clear mind. This belief is reflected in myths where amethyst is associated with Dionysus, the god of wine. According to one tale, amethyst was created when the goddess Artemis transformed a nymph into a quartz crystal to shield her from Dionysus' unwanted advances. The god, remorseful, poured wine over the crystal, dyeing it a beautiful purple.

Throughout history, amethyst has been revered for its spiritual significance. In ancient Egypt, it was carved into amulets for protection and worn by royalty as a symbol of power and status. It was also used in burial rituals to guide the deceased on their journey to the afterlife. Medieval European soldiers wore amethyst talismans for protection in battle, believing the stone could calm their minds and enhance courage. Tibetan monks still use amethyst in meditation to achieve higher states of consciousness.

Amethyst's metaphysical properties are closely linked to its vibrant violet colour. Violet is associated with the crown chakra, the energy center located at the top of the head. This chakra governs our spiritual connection and higher awareness. By working with amethyst, we can stimulate and balance the crown chakra, leading to enhanced intuition, spiritual insights, and a deeper connection to our inner wisdom.

One of amethyst's most celebrated benefits is its ability to promote inner peace and tranquility. Its calming energy helps to alleviate stress, anxiety, and emotional turmoil. Holding an amethyst crystal or placing it on the forehead can create a sense of serenity, allowing us to let go of worries and find solace in the present moment. Meditation with amethyst can further deepen this relaxation response, facilitating a sense of inner peace that extends beyond the meditation session.

Amethyst is also believed to strengthen intuition and psychic abilities. It can sharpen our perception, making us more attuned to subtle energies and messages from the universe. This heightened intuition can guide us in making decisions, navigating challenges, and uncovering hidden truths. Amethyst can be particularly helpful for those seeking to develop their spiritual gifts or embark on a path of self-discovery.

In addition to its spiritual benefits, amethyst is thought to have physical healing properties. It's been used to soothe headaches, promote restful sleep, and relieve physical tension. Amethyst is also said to support the immune system, strengthen the endocrine system, and aid in detoxification. Whether or not you believe in the science behind these claims, the placebo effect of holding a beautiful crystal and focusing on positive outcomes can be powerful in itself.

To experience the full benefits of amethyst, there are various ways to incorporate it into your life. Wearing amethyst jewellery allows the stone's energy to resonate with your personal energy field throughout the day. Keeping amethyst crystals in your home or workspace can create a calming and uplifting atmosphere. Meditating with amethyst can deepen your spiritual practice and enhance your intuitive abilities. You can also place amethyst under your pillow to promote peaceful sleep and vivid dreams.

Amethyst, with its captivating beauty and profound spiritual significance, is a true gem in the world of crystals. Its ability to foster inner peace, intuition, and spiritual connection makes it a valuable tool for personal growth and well-being. Whether you're drawn to amethyst for its aesthetic appeal, its historical significance, or its metaphysical properties, this "stone of serenity" has the potential to transform your life and guide you on a path of inner peace and spiritual awakening.

ᗐᗐᗐ

Amethyst whispers serenity, calming the storms within and guiding the soul towards inner tranquility. Embrace its violet embrace, and find solace in its peaceful presence.

TWO
ROSE QUARTZ: LOVE AND COMPASSION. SUBTITLE: EMBRACE UNCONDITIONAL AFFECTION.

Rose Quartz, a delicate gemstone with a gentle pink hue, embodies the essence of love and compassion. It is a stone that whispers of unconditional affection and invites us to open our hearts to the boundless possibilities of love in all its forms. Let's journey through the captivating world of Rose Quartz and discover how it can nurture compassion, healing, and the embrace of unconditional love within ourselves and others.

The name "Rose Quartz" aptly reflects its soft pink colour, reminiscent of a blushing rose. This colour is associated with the heart chakra, the energy center located in the center of the chest. The heart chakra governs our emotions, relationships, and ability to give and receive love. Rose Quartz is believed to resonate with the heart chakra, stimulating its energy flow and fostering emotional healing, compassion, and love for ourselves and others.

Rose Quartz has a rich history intertwined with various cultures and traditions. In ancient Egypt, it was cherished for its beauty-enhancing properties and used in facial masks and elixirs. It was also associated with the goddess Isis, a symbol of feminine power and love. In Greek mythology, Rose Quartz is linked to Aphrodite, the goddess of love and beauty, and believed to have been created from her tears and the blood of her lover, Adonis. Throughout history, Rose Quartz has been treasured as a talisman for love, promoting harmony in relationships and attracting romantic partners.

One of the most profound qualities of Rose Quartz is its association with unconditional love. Unlike romantic love, which can be conditional and fleeting, unconditional love is a pure and limitless form of affection that accepts and cherishes without judgment or expectation. Rose Quartz encourages us to embrace this form of love, not only for others but also for ourselves. By cultivating self-love, we can heal emotional wounds, boost self-esteem, and establish healthier relationships with others.

Rose Quartz is a powerful ally in emotional healing. It can help us to release past traumas, forgive ourselves and others, and let go of negative emotions such as anger, resentment, and grief. Its soothing energy comforts and supports us through difficult times, reminding us of our inherent worthiness and capacity for love. By working with Rose Quartz, we can cultivate a sense of inner peace and emotional resilience that allows us to navigate life's challenges with grace and compassion.

Compassion, the ability to understand and share the feelings of others, is another key attribute associated with Rose Quartz. It encourages us to step into the shoes of others, to see the world through their eyes, and to respond with empathy and kindness. This heightened sense of compassion extends not only to our loved ones but also to strangers, animals, and the environment. By practicing compassion, we create a ripple effect of love and understanding that can transform our relationships and communities.

Rose Quartz is also believed to promote harmony and understanding in relationships. It can help to strengthen existing bonds, mend broken hearts, and attract new love into our lives. By placing Rose Quartz in the bedroom or wearing it as jewellery, we can invite its loving energy into our relationships, fostering intimacy, communication, and mutual respect.

In addition to its emotional and relational benefits, Rose Quartz is thought to have physical healing properties. It is often used to support heart health, promote circulation, and soothe skin conditions. Some believe that Rose Quartz can even aid in fertility and pregnancy. While scientific evidence supporting these claims is limited, the placebo effect of working with Rose Quartz and focusing on positive outcomes can be powerful in itself.

To experience the transformative power of Rose Quartz, there are many ways to incorporate it into your daily life. Wearing Rose Quartz jewellery allows you to carry its loving energy with you wherever you go. Placing Rose Quartz in your home or workspace can create a calming and harmonious environment. Meditating with Rose Quartz can deepen your connection to your heart center and enhance your ability to give and receive love. You can also use Rose Quartz in crystal grids, elixirs, or simply hold it in your hand while setting intentions for love, compassion, and healing.

Rose Quartz, with its gentle pink glow and loving energy, is a true gift from the Earth. Its ability to nurture self-love, compassion, and emotional healing makes it an invaluable tool for personal growth and well-being. Whether you're seeking to mend a broken heart, deepen your relationships, or simply cultivate more love and compassion in your life, Rose Quartz is a powerful ally that can guide you on a journey of self-discovery and unconditional love.

ϷϷϷ

Rose Quartz, a gentle caress of the heart, opens us to the boundless depths of love. Let its tender energy wash over you, and discover the healing power of unconditional affection.

THREE

CLEAR QUARTZ: AMPLIFICATION AND CLARITY. SUBTITLE: THE MASTER HEALER.

Clear Quartz, a crystalline marvel with a pristine clarity, has long been revered as the "master healer" in the realm of gemstones. Its remarkable ability to amplify energy and promote clarity has made it a cornerstone of crystal healing practices and a cherished tool for spiritual seekers. Let us embark on a journey into the depths of Clear Quartz, exploring its captivating properties, historical significance, and its profound impact on our well-being.

The name "Clear Quartz" perfectly encapsulates its most striking feature: its exceptional clarity. Unlike other gemstones that boast vibrant colours, Clear Quartz is transparent, allowing light to pass through it unimpeded. This transparency symbolizes purity, clarity of thought, and the ability to see through illusions. Clear Quartz is composed of silicon dioxide, one of the most abundant minerals on Earth. Its crystal structure is a hexagonal prism, often terminating in a pyramidal point, reflecting its association with focused energy and direction.

Clear Quartz has a rich history that spans cultures and continents. In ancient civilizations, it was believed to be a gift from the gods, embodying divine light and wisdom. Native American shamans used Clear Quartz in healing rituals, while ancient Egyptians carved it into amulets for protection and spiritual guidance. In many cultures, Clear Quartz was revered as a symbol of clarity, purity, and connection to the spiritual realm. Its use in divination and prophecy further solidified its association with heightened awareness and intuitive insights.

One of the most remarkable properties of Clear Quartz is its ability to amplify energy. It acts as a natural amplifier, enhancing the energy of other crystals and intentions. This makes it an indispensable tool in crystal healing, where it is often used in conjunction with other gemstones to maximize their therapeutic effects. When programmed with a specific intention, Clear Quartz can focus and direct that energy towards a desired outcome, whether it be healing, manifestation, or personal growth.

Clear Quartz is also renowned for its ability to promote clarity of mind. Its pure and focused energy helps to dispel mental fog, confusion, and negative thought patterns. By working with Clear Quartz, we can gain clarity on our goals, make decisions with greater ease, and connect with our inner wisdom. It is often used in meditation to quiet the mind, enhance focus, and access higher states of consciousness.

Another key attribute of Clear Quartz is its ability to cleanse and purify energy. It acts as a natural filter, absorbing, neutralizing, and transmuting negative energies. This makes it a valuable tool for clearing spaces, auras, and even the energy of other crystals. By regularly cleansing our energy field with Clear Quartz, we can maintain a sense of balance and harmony, preventing the accumulation of negativity that can lead to physical and emotional dis-ease.

Clear Quartz is a versatile crystal that can be used in a variety of ways. Wearing it as jewellery allows its energy to resonate with your personal energy field throughout the day. Keeping Clear Quartz crystals in your home or workspace can create a more positive and energized environment. Meditating with Clear Quartz can deepen your spiritual practice and enhance your connection to your higher self. You can also use Clear Quartz in crystal grids, elixirs, or simply hold it in your hand while setting intentions for clarity, healing, or manifestation.

Clear Quartz, with its pristine clarity and powerful energy, is a true gift from the Earth. Its ability to amplify, clarify, and purify energy makes it an invaluable tool for personal growth, spiritual development, and holistic healing. Whether you're a seasoned crystal enthusiast or new to the world of gemstones, Clear Quartz is a must-have addition to your crystal collection. Its versatility and profound benefits make it a true "master healer" that can support you on your journey towards greater clarity, well-being, and spiritual awakening.

Remember, the true power of Clear Quartz lies not only in its inherent properties but also in your intention and connection to its energy. By approaching Clear Quartz with an open heart and a clear mind, you can unlock its full potential and experience its transformative effects on your life.

ϸϸϸ

Clear Quartz, a beacon of light, amplifies intention and illuminates the path to clarity. Harness its energy, and let it magnify your desires, dreams, and aspirations.

FOUR

CITRINE: ABUNDANCE AND PROSPERITY. SUBTITLE: ATTRACT JOY AND SUCCESS.

Citrine, a radiant gemstone with its sunny yellow to golden hues, is often hailed as the "stone of abundance and prosperity." It evokes feelings of joy, optimism, and success, attracting positive energy and opportunities into our lives. Let's embark on a journey through the vibrant world of Citrine and discover how it can ignite our inner light, attract abundance, and pave the way for a life filled with joy and success.

The name "Citrine" is derived from the French word "citron," meaning "lemon." This aptly describes its bright yellow colour, reminiscent of sunshine and citrus fruits. Citrine is a variety of quartz that gets its colour from trace amounts of iron. Its vibrant yellow to golden shades are associated with the solar plexus chakra, the energy center located just above the navel. The solar plexus chakra governs our personal power, self-esteem, and sense of purpose. By working with Citrine, we can stimulate and balance this chakra, empowering us to manifest our desires and achieve our goals.

Citrine has a long history of being associated with abundance and prosperity. In ancient times, it was believed to bring good fortune to merchants and traders, leading to its nickname as the "merchant's stone." It was often carried as a talisman to attract wealth and success in business ventures. In Chinese Feng Shui, Citrine is placed in the wealth corner of a home or office to attract financial prosperity and abundance. The ancient Greeks also valued Citrine for its ability to bring joy, happiness, and positive energy into their lives.

One of the most celebrated properties of Citrine is its ability to attract abundance and prosperity into our lives. It is believed to open our minds to new possibilities, attract opportunities, and enhance our creativity and resourcefulness. By working with Citrine, we can shift our mindset from scarcity to abundance, allowing us to see the unlimited potential that surrounds us. It encourages us to take action towards our goals, trust in the universe's abundance, and embrace the flow of prosperity into our lives.

Citrine is also a powerful stone for manifesting our desires. It helps us to clarify our intentions, visualize our goals, and take inspired action towards their realization. By programming Citrine with our specific desires, we can amplify their energy and attract the resources and opportunities needed to manifest them into reality. Citrine reminds us that we are co-creators of our reality and that our thoughts and actions have the power to shape our lives.

In addition to attracting material abundance, Citrine is also associated with attracting joy and happiness into our lives. Its vibrant energy uplifts our spirits, dispels negativity, and promotes a sense of optimism and enthusiasm. By surrounding ourselves with Citrine, we can cultivate a joyful and positive outlook on life, attract like-minded people, and create experiences that bring us happiness and fulfillment.

Citrine is a wonderful tool for boosting self-confidence and self-esteem. It helps us to recognize our own strengths, talents, and potential. By working with Citrine, we can overcome self-doubt, embrace our unique gifts, and shine our light in the world. This increased self-confidence can empower us to take on new challenges, pursue our passions, and achieve our dreams.

Beyond its metaphysical properties, Citrine is also believed to have physical healing benefits. It is often used to support digestion, stimulate metabolism, and detoxify the body. Citrine is also said to enhance creativity, improve mental clarity, and strengthen the immune system. While scientific evidence for these claims is limited, the power of intention and the placebo effect can be significant in the healing process.

To harness the transformative energy of Citrine, there are several ways to incorporate it into your daily life. Wearing Citrine jewellery allows you to carry its vibrant energy with you wherever you go. Placing Citrine in your home or workspace can create an atmosphere of abundance, joy, and success. Meditating with Citrine can help you to connect with your inner power, visualize your goals, and attract positive energy into your life. You can also use Citrine in crystal grids, carry it in your pocket, or simply hold it in your hand while setting intentions for abundance, prosperity, and joy.

Citrine, with its radiant glow and uplifting energy, is a true treasure from the Earth. Its ability to attract abundance, promote joy, and empower us to manifest our dreams makes it an invaluable tool for personal growth and well-being. Whether you're seeking financial prosperity, career success, or simply a more joyful and fulfilling life, Citrine is a powerful ally that can guide you on your path towards abundance and success.

Remember, the true power of Citrine lies not only in its inherent properties but also in your belief and intention. By approaching Citrine with an open heart and a positive mindset, you can unlock its full potential and experience the transformative effects it can have on your life. So, let the radiant energy of Citrine illuminate your path and guide you towards a life filled with abundance, joy, and success.

ppp

Citrine radiates the golden warmth of abundance and prosperity. Bask in its sunny embrace, and let its energy attract joy, success, and endless possibilities into your life.

FIVE

TIGER'S EYE: GROUNDING AND PROTECTION. SUBTITLE: HARNESS COURAGE AND STRENGTH.

Tiger's Eye, a mesmerizing gemstone with its shimmering golden-brown bands and silky luster, has been revered for centuries as a stone of grounding, protection, and inner strength. Its captivating appearance, reminiscent of a tiger's eye, evokes a sense of courage, resilience, and unwavering focus. Let's delve into the enchanting world of Tiger's Eye and explore how it can empower us to harness our inner strength, face challenges with courage, and stay grounded in the present moment.

Tiger's Eye is a chatoyant gemstone, meaning it exhibits a luminous band of reflected light that seems to shift and shimmer as the stone is moved. This captivating optical effect, known as chatoyancy, is caused by the parallel arrangement of fibrous inclusions within the stone. These inclusions, often composed of crocidolite or asbestos fibers, create the characteristic golden-brown bands and silky luster that give Tiger's Eye its unique allure.

The name "Tiger's Eye" reflects its resemblance to the eye of a tiger, a symbol of power, courage, and protection in many cultures. In ancient Egypt, Tiger's Eye was associated with the sun god Ra, believed to provide protection from evil spirits and negative energies. Roman soldiers wore Tiger's Eye talismans for courage and strength in battle. In Chinese culture, it is considered a stone of good fortune and prosperity, often used in Feng Shui practices to attract wealth and abundance.

One of the most remarkable properties of Tiger's Eye is its grounding energy. It is a stone that connects us to the earth, helping us to feel stable, secure, and rooted in the present moment. In today's fast-paced world, where we are constantly bombarded with information and distractions, it can be easy to feel ungrounded and disconnected from our bodies and the natural world. Tiger's Eye reminds us of our connection to the earth, helping us to stay centered and focused, even in the midst of chaos.

Tiger's Eye is also a stone of protection. It is believed to create a shield of positive energy around us, deflecting negative influences and protecting us from harm. This can be especially beneficial for those who are sensitive to energy or who work in environments where they are exposed to negativity. Tiger's Eye can also help to strengthen our personal boundaries, making it easier to say no and protect our energy from those who would drain or deplete it.

Another key attribute of Tiger's Eye is its ability to enhance courage and strength. It is a stone that empowers us to face our fears, overcome challenges, and step into our personal power. Tiger's Eye can help us to cultivate a sense of inner strength and resilience, allowing us to persevere through difficult times and emerge stronger on the other side. It is a stone that reminds us that we have the courage and strength within us to achieve our goals and live our lives to the fullest.

Tiger's Eye is also believed to stimulate creativity and problem-solving abilities. It helps us to see things from a new perspective, find innovative solutions, and tap into our intuition. This can be particularly helpful for those who are feeling stuck or creatively blocked. Tiger's Eye can also help us to focus our energy and attention, making it easier to complete tasks and achieve our goals.

In addition to its metaphysical properties, Tiger's Eye is thought to have physical healing benefits. It is often used to improve circulation, alleviate pain, and strengthen the bones and joints. Tiger's Eye is also said to support the digestive system, boost energy levels, and enhance overall vitality. While scientific evidence for these claims is limited, the power of intention and the placebo effect can be significant in the healing process.

To harness the transformative energy of Tiger's Eye, there are several ways to incorporate it into your daily life. Wearing Tiger's Eye jewellery allows you to carry its grounding and protective energy with you wherever you go. Placing Tiger's Eye in your home or workspace can create a more stable, secure, and energized environment. Meditating with Tiger's Eye can help you to connect with your inner strength, release fear and anxiety, and cultivate courage. You can also use Tiger's Eye in crystal grids, carry it in your pocket, or simply hold it in your hand while setting intentions for grounding, protection, and inner strength.

Tiger's Eye, with its captivating beauty and powerful energy, is a true gift from the Earth. Its ability to ground us, protect us, and empower us to harness our inner strength makes it an invaluable tool for personal growth, spiritual development, and overall well-being. Whether you're facing a challenging situation, seeking to boost your confidence, or simply want to feel more grounded and centered in your daily life, Tiger's Eye is a powerful ally that can support you on your journey.

Remember, the true power of Tiger's Eye lies not only in its inherent properties but also in your connection to its energy. By approaching Tiger's Eye with an open heart and a willingness to explore its depths, you can unlock its full potential and experience the transformative effects it can have on your life. So, let the shimmering energy of Tiger's Eye ignite your courage, strengthen your resolve, and guide you towards a life filled with confidence, resilience, and unwavering inner strength.

Tiger's Eye, a guardian of strength and courage, shields us from negativity and empowers us to face our fears. With its watchful eye, we can conquer challenges and walk our path with confidence.

SIX

SODALITE: COMMUNICATION AND TRUTH. SUBTITLE: SPEAK YOUR MIND WITH CONFIDENCE.

Sodalite, a captivating gemstone with its deep blue hues and intricate white veining, is a stone of communication, truth, and inner wisdom. Its calming energy encourages self-expression, enhances intuition, and promotes harmony in relationships. Let's embark on a journey into the depths of Sodalite and explore how it can empower us to speak our minds with confidence, connect with our inner truth, and foster harmonious communication with others.

The name "Sodalite" derives from its sodium content, as "soda" refers to sodium in mineralogy. This vibrant blue stone is often found in volcanic rocks and is known for its unique patterns and colour variations. Sodalite's deep blue colour is associated with the throat chakra, the energy center located in the throat. The throat chakra governs communication, self-expression, and our ability to speak our truth. By working with Sodalite, we can stimulate and balance this chakra, enhancing our communication skills, promoting self-expression, and fostering honest and authentic interactions.

Sodalite has a rich history intertwined with various cultures and traditions. In ancient Egypt, it was used in amulets and jewellery for protection and spiritual guidance. The Egyptians believed that Sodalite could enhance intuition and psychic abilities, allowing them to connect with higher realms of consciousness. In the Middle Ages, Sodalite was used in religious art and architecture, symbolizing wisdom, truth, and divine inspiration. The Incas also valued Sodalite for its metaphysical properties, using it in healing rituals and ceremonies to promote peace, harmony, and understanding.

One of the most profound qualities of Sodalite is its association with communication and self-expression. It is a stone that empowers us to speak our minds with confidence, clarity, and authenticity. It helps us to articulate our thoughts and feelings clearly, express our needs and desires effectively, and communicate our truth with compassion and understanding. Sodalite can be particularly helpful for those who struggle with shyness, social anxiety, or difficulty expressing themselves in certain situations.

Sodalite is also a stone of truth. It encourages us to seek and embrace our own truth, even when it is uncomfortable or challenging. It helps us to see through illusions, dispel self-doubt, and trust in our own inner knowing. By connecting with our truth, we can live more authentically, make decisions that align with our values, and create a life that is true to our authentic selves.

Another key attribute of Sodalite is its ability to enhance intuition and insight. It is believed to stimulate the third eye chakra, the energy center located between the eyebrows, which governs our intuition, insight, and spiritual awareness. By working with Sodalite, we can tap into our inner wisdom, gain clarity on our life path, and make decisions that are aligned with our highest good. It can also help us to connect with our spirit guides, access higher realms of consciousness, and receive divine guidance.

Sodalite is also a stone of harmony and unity. It promotes understanding, compassion, and cooperation in relationships. By wearing or carrying Sodalite, we can foster open and honest communication with our loved ones, resolve conflicts peacefully, and create a more harmonious and supportive environment. Sodalite can also help to strengthen group dynamics, enhance teamwork, and promote a sense of unity and common purpose.

In addition to its metaphysical properties, Sodalite is believed to have physical healing benefits. It is often used to soothe sore throats, reduce inflammation, and boost the immune system. Sodalite is also said to regulate blood pressure, improve sleep, and alleviate headaches and migraines. While scientific evidence for these claims is limited, the power of intention and the placebo effect can be significant in the healing process.

To harness the transformative energy of Sodalite, there are several ways to incorporate it into your daily life. Wearing Sodalite jewellery allows you to carry its calming and empowering energy with you wherever you go. Placing Sodalite in your home or workspace can create an atmosphere of peace, harmony, and clear communication. Meditating with Sodalite can help you to connect with your inner truth, enhance your intuition, and strengthen your communication skills. You can also use Sodalite in crystal grids, elixirs, or simply hold it in your hand while setting intentions for clear communication, truth, and harmonious relationships.

Sodalite, with its mesmerizing beauty and profound metaphysical properties, is a true gem in the world of crystals. Its ability to enhance communication, promote truth, and foster harmonious relationships makes it a valuable tool for personal growth and well-being. Whether you're seeking to improve your communication skills, connect with your inner truth, or create more harmonious relationships, Sodalite is a powerful ally that can guide you on your journey towards greater authenticity, self-expression, and understanding.

Remember, the true power of Sodalite lies not only in its inherent properties but also in your connection to its energy and your intention to utilize its gifts. By approaching Sodalite with an open heart and a willingness to embrace its wisdom, you can unlock its full potential and experience its transformative effects on your communication, relationships, and overall well-being. So, let the calming blue energy of Sodalite guide you towards a life filled with clear communication, authentic self-expression, and harmonious relationships.

ϸϸϸ

Sodalite, a whisper of truth, encourages authentic expression and deepens our understanding of self. Embrace its calming blue, and let your voice ring out with clarity and conviction.

SEVEN

CARNELIAN: CREATIVITY AND VITALITY. SUBTITLE: IGNITE PASSION AND MOTIVATION.

Carnelian, a vibrant gemstone with hues ranging from fiery orange to deep reddish-brown, is a stone of creativity, vitality, and passion. Its warm and energizing energy ignites the spark of inspiration, fuels motivation, and encourages us to embrace our creative potential. Let's delve into the captivating world of Carnelian and explore how it can awaken our passions, enhance our vitality, and unleash our creative expression.

The name "Carnelian" is believed to derive from the Latin word "carnis," meaning "flesh," referring to its reddish colour. This warm and vibrant hue is associated with the sacral chakra, the energy center located below the navel. The sacral chakra governs our creativity, sexuality, passion, and life force energy. By working with

Carnelian, we can stimulate and balance this chakra, enhancing our creative expression, boosting our vitality, and igniting our passions.

Carnelian has a rich history intertwined with various cultures and traditions. In ancient Egypt, it was associated with the goddess Isis, a symbol of feminine power and fertility. Carnelian amulets were often worn to protect against negative energies and promote vitality and abundance. The ancient Romans also valued Carnelian for its protective qualities and used it in jewellery and talismans. In the Middle Ages, Carnelian was believed to enhance courage, passion, and leadership qualities. It was also used in healing practices to improve blood circulation, increase energy levels, and promote overall well-being.

One of the most remarkable properties of Carnelian is its ability to stimulate creativity and inspiration. It is a stone that awakens our inner artist, encouraging us to explore our creative potential and express ourselves authentically. Carnelian can help us to overcome creative blocks, tap into our imagination, and bring our ideas to life. It is a powerful tool for artists, writers, musicians, and anyone who seeks to unleash their creative spirit.

Carnelian is also a stone of vitality and passion. It invigorates our physical and emotional energy, boosting our stamina, motivation, and enthusiasm for life. It helps us to overcome lethargy, procrastination, and self-doubt, empowering us to take action towards our goals and pursue our passions with renewed vigor. Carnelian reminds us that life is meant to be lived fully and encourages us to embrace our zest for life.

Another key attribute of Carnelian is its association with sexuality and sensuality. It is believed to enhance libido, promote fertility, and deepen intimacy in relationships. Carnelian can also help to heal emotional wounds related to sexuality and intimacy, allowing us to embrace our sensual nature with confidence and joy. It is a stone that celebrates the sacredness of sexuality and reminds us of the power of love and connection.

Carnelian is also a stone of courage and confidence. It helps us to overcome fears, take risks, and step out of our comfort zones. It empowers us to stand up for ourselves, speak our truth, and pursue our dreams with unwavering determination. Carnelian can be particularly helpful for those who struggle with self-doubt, shyness, or a lack of motivation. It is a stone that reminds us of our inner strength and encourages us to live life boldly and passionately.

In addition to its metaphysical properties, Carnelian is believed to have physical healing benefits. It is often used to improve circulation, boost energy levels, and strengthen the immune system. Carnelian is also said to support reproductive health, alleviate menstrual cramps, and promote healthy digestion. While scientific evidence for these claims is limited, the power of intention and the placebo effect can be significant in the healing process.

To harness the transformative energy of Carnelian, there are many ways to incorporate it into your daily life. Wearing Carnelian jewellery allows you to carry its vibrant energy with you wherever you go. Placing Carnelian in your home or workspace can create a more creative, energized, and passionate atmosphere. Meditating with Carnelian can help you to connect with your inner fire, ignite your passions, and unleash your creative potential. You can also use Carnelian in crystal grids, elixirs, or simply hold it in your hand while setting intentions for creativity, vitality, and passion.

Carnelian, with its fiery energy and vibrant hues, is a true gift from the Earth. Its ability to stimulate creativity, enhance vitality, and ignite passion makes it an invaluable tool for personal growth and well-being. Whether you're an artist seeking inspiration, a dreamer yearning to bring your visions to life, or simply someone who wants to live life more fully and passionately, Carnelian is a powerful ally that can guide you on your journey.

Remember, the true power of Carnelian lies not only in its inherent properties but also in your connection to its energy and your willingness to embrace its vibrant spirit. By approaching Carnelian with an open heart and a fiery spirit, you can unlock its full potential and experience its transformative effects on your creativity, vitality, and passion for life. So, let the warm and energizing energy of Carnelian ignite your passions, awaken your creative spirit, and empower you to live life to the fullest.

ᗄᗄᗄ

Carnelian, a spark of creativity and passion, ignites our inner fire and fuels our creative expression. Unleash its vibrant energy, and let your passions guide you towards a life of fulfillment.

EIGHT

MOONSTONE: FEMININE ENERGY AND NEW BEGINNINGS. SUBTITLE: EMBRACE CYCLES AND CHANGE.

Moonstone, a gemstone with an ethereal glow and iridescent shimmer, embodies the essence of feminine energy, new beginnings, and the cyclical nature of life. Its alluring beauty and mystical properties have captivated cultures across the ages, drawing us into a realm of intuition, emotional healing, and harmonious cycles. Let us delve into the enchanting world of Moonstone and explore how it can empower us to embrace change, connect with our feminine energy, and flow with the natural rhythms of life.

The name "Moonstone" perfectly reflects its connection to the moon, the celestial body that governs the tides, emotions, and the cycles of life. Moonstone's characteristic adularescence, a shimmering play of light within the stone, is reminiscent of the moon's gentle glow. This phenomenon is caused by the intergrowth of two different types of feldspar within the stone, which scatters light and creates the illusion of a floating glow. The colours of Moonstone can range from milky white to peach, blue, gray, and even rainbow hues, each with its own unique energy and symbolism.

Moonstone has a rich history intertwined with various cultures and spiritual traditions. In ancient India, it was believed to be formed from solidified moonbeams and was associated with divine feminine energy and fertility. It was often used in jewellery and amulets to promote fertility, protect women during childbirth, and enhance intuition. In Roman mythology, Moonstone was linked to the goddess Diana, the goddess of the moon, hunting, and childbirth. It was believed to bring good fortune, protect travelers, and enhance psychic abilities. Throughout history, Moonstone has been revered as a talisman for feminine energy, intuition, and emotional balance.

One of the most profound qualities of Moonstone is its association with feminine energy. It resonates with the divine feminine, the archetypal energy of creation, nurturing, intuition, and emotional depth. By working with Moonstone, we can connect with and embrace our feminine energy, regardless of our gender identity. This can help us to cultivate greater self-acceptance, compassion, intuition, and emotional intelligence. Moonstone can be particularly supportive for women during times of hormonal fluctuations, pregnancy, and menopause, helping to balance emotions, ease menstrual discomfort, and promote overall well-being.

Moonstone is also a stone of new beginnings. It encourages us to embrace change, release old patterns, and step into new phases of our lives with confidence and grace. It helps us to trust in the natural cycles of life, knowing that endings are always followed by new beginnings. Moonstone can be a powerful ally during times of transition, such as starting a new job, moving to a new home, or ending a relationship. It can help us to navigate these changes with greater ease, find new opportunities for growth, and embrace the unknown with open hearts.

Another key attribute of Moonstone is its connection to intuition and psychic abilities. It is believed to enhance our intuitive powers, allowing us to tap into our inner knowing and receive guidance from higher realms. Moonstone can help us to trust our gut feelings, make decisions with confidence, and navigate life's challenges with greater clarity and insight. It is a powerful tool for those seeking to develop their psychic abilities, deepen their spiritual practice, and connect with their inner wisdom.

Moonstone is also a stone of emotional healing. It helps us to release emotional baggage, heal past traumas, and cultivate a greater sense of emotional balance and well-being. Its calming and soothing energy can alleviate stress, anxiety, and emotional turmoil, allowing us to find inner peace and tranquility. Moonstone can also help us to connect with our emotions, understand their origins, and process them in a healthy and constructive way.

In addition to its metaphysical properties, Moonstone is thought to have physical healing benefits. It is often used to regulate hormonal cycles, ease menstrual discomfort, and promote fertility. Moonstone is also said to support digestion, improve sleep, and alleviate headaches and migraines. While scientific evidence for these claims is limited, the power of intention and the placebo effect can be significant in the healing process.

To harness the transformative energy of Moonstone, there are many ways to incorporate it into your daily life. Wearing Moonstone jewellery allows you to carry its gentle and nurturing energy with you wherever you go. Placing Moonstone in your home or bedroom can create a calming and serene atmosphere. Meditating with Moonstone can deepen your connection to your intuition, emotions, and the divine feminine. You can also use Moonstone in crystal grids, elixirs, or simply hold it in your hand while setting intentions for emotional healing, new beginnings, and embracing the cycles of life.

Moonstone, with its ethereal glow and mystical properties, is a true gift from the Earth. Its ability to connect us with our feminine energy, embrace change, and foster emotional healing makes it an invaluable tool for personal growth and well-being. Whether you're seeking to balance your emotions, embark on a new chapter in your life, or simply deepen your connection to the divine feminine, Moonstone is a powerful ally that can guide you on your journey towards greater self-awareness, intuition, and emotional well-being. Remember, the true power of Moonstone lies not only in its inherent properties but also in your connection to its energy and your willingness to embrace the cyclical nature of life. By approaching Moonstone with an open heart and a willingness to surrender to the flow of life, you can unlock its full potential and experience its transformative effects on your emotional, spiritual, and physical well-being.

ᚦᚦᚦ

Moonstone, a luminous pearl of feminine energy, embraces the cycles of life and nurtures our intuition. Bathe in its gentle glow, and find balance and harmony within.

NINE
LAPIS LAZULI: WISDOM AND SELF-EXPRESSION. SUBTITLE: AWAKEN INNER VISION.

Lapis Lazuli, an exquisite gemstone with its deep, celestial blue colour speckled with golden pyrite, has been revered for millennia as a stone of wisdom, truth, and self-expression. Its captivating beauty and powerful metaphysical properties have drawn seekers of knowledge and spiritual enlightenment to its depths for centuries. Let us embark on a journey into the mystical world of Lapis Lazuli and explore how it can awaken our inner vision, enhance our communication, and unlock the wisdom that resides within.

The name "Lapis Lazuli" originates from Latin and Persian origins. "Lapis" is Latin for "stone," while "lazuli" comes from the Persian word "lazaward," meaning "blue." This aptly describes the gemstone's striking blue colour, reminiscent of the night sky adorned with shimmering stars. The golden flecks of pyrite within Lapis Lazuli are often likened to the celestial bodies that illuminate the heavens, further enhancing its association with cosmic wisdom and spiritual enlightenment.

Lapis Lazuli has a rich and storied history that spans cultures and continents. In ancient Egypt, it was considered a sacred stone associated with the goddess Isis, a symbol of divine wisdom and power. Lapis Lazuli was used in jewellery, amulets, and even ground into pigments for cosmetics and artwork. The Egyptians believed that Lapis Lazuli could enhance psychic abilities, facilitate communication with the gods, and protect against negative energies. In Mesopotamia, it was used to create cylinder seals, which were used to mark official documents and authenticate transactions. In the Middle Ages, Lapis Lazuli was highly valued by artists and craftsmen, who used it to create intricate mosaics and illuminate manuscripts.

One of the most profound qualities of Lapis Lazuli is its association with wisdom and truth. It is a stone that stimulates the mind, enhances intellectual clarity, and expands our understanding of ourselves and the world around us. By working with Lapis Lazuli, we can tap into our inner wisdom, gain insights into our life purpose, and make decisions that align with our higher truth. It is a powerful tool for students, scholars, and anyone seeking to deepen their knowledge and expand their consciousness.

Lapis Lazuli is also a stone of self-expression and communication. It empowers us to speak our truth with confidence, clarity, and conviction. It helps us to articulate our thoughts and feelings effectively, express our creativity, and communicate our ideas with impact. By wearing or carrying Lapis Lazuli, we can enhance our communication skills, improve our public speaking abilities, and express ourselves authentically.

Another key attribute of Lapis Lazuli is its ability to awaken our inner vision. It is believed to stimulate the third eye chakra, the energy center located between the eyebrows, which governs our intuition, insight, and spiritual awareness. By working with Lapis Lazuli, we can enhance our intuitive abilities, access higher realms of consciousness, and receive divine guidance. It can also help us to see through illusions, discern truth from falsehood, and make decisions based on our inner knowing.

Lapis Lazuli is also a stone of spiritual growth and enlightenment. It helps us to connect with our higher selves, deepen our spiritual practice, and embark on a journey of self-discovery. By meditating with Lapis Lazuli, we can quiet the mind, expand our awareness, and access higher states of consciousness. It is a powerful tool for those seeking to connect with their spiritual guides, receive divine inspiration, and awaken their spiritual potential.

In addition to its metaphysical properties, Lapis Lazuli is thought to have physical healing benefits. It is often used to alleviate headaches, soothe insomnia, and boost the immune system. Lapis Lazuli is also said to support respiratory health, improve blood circulation, and enhance overall vitality. While scientific evidence for these claims is limited, the power of intention and the placebo effect can be significant in the healing process.

To harness the transformative energy of Lapis Lazuli, there are several ways to incorporate it into your daily life. Wearing Lapis Lazuli jewellery allows you to carry its wisdom and energy with you wherever you go. Placing Lapis Lazuli in your home or workspace can create an atmosphere conducive to intellectual pursuits, creative expression, and spiritual growth. Meditating with Lapis Lazuli can deepen your spiritual practice, enhance your intuition, and connect you with your inner wisdom. You can also use Lapis Lazuli in crystal grids, elixirs, or simply hold it in your hand while setting intentions for wisdom, self-expression, and spiritual enlightenment.

Lapis Lazuli, with its celestial blue hues and golden specks, is a true gem in the world of crystals. Its ability to awaken our inner vision, enhance our communication, and unlock our wisdom makes it an invaluable tool for personal growth, spiritual development, and self-expression. Whether you're a seeker of knowledge, a creative soul, or someone seeking to deepen their spiritual connection, Lapis Lazuli is a powerful ally that can guide you on your journey towards greater self-awareness, wisdom, and authentic expression. Remember, the true power of Lapis Lazuli lies not only in its inherent properties but also in your connection to its energy and your intention to utilize its gifts. By approaching Lapis Lazuli with an open heart and a thirst for knowledge, you can unlock its full potential and experience its transformative effects on your mind, body, and spirit.

ᗁᗁᗁ

Lapis Lazuli, a window to the soul, unlocks the wisdom within and reveals our true potential. Gaze into its depths, and let its celestial blue guide you towards enlightenment and self-discovery.

TEN

OBSIDIAN: TRANSFORMATION AND RELEASE. SUBTITLE: SHATTER ILLUSIONS, UNCOVER TRUTH.

Obsidian, a striking volcanic glass with its deep, inky blackness and glassy sheen, has long been revered as a stone of transformation, protection, and truth. Its enigmatic beauty and powerful metaphysical properties have drawn those seeking self-discovery, healing, and spiritual growth to its depths for centuries. Let us embark on a journey into the mysterious world of Obsidian and explore how it can shatter illusions, uncover hidden truths, and facilitate profound personal transformation.

Obsidian's name is believed to have originated from Obsius, a Roman explorer who is said to have discovered the stone in

Ethiopia. It is formed when volcanic lava cools rapidly, resulting in a glass-like structure with minimal crystal growth. This unique formation gives Obsidian its characteristic smooth texture, sharp edges, and vitreous luster. Its colour can range from jet black to deep brown, gray, or even iridescent shades, depending on its mineral composition and cooling process.

Throughout history, Obsidian has been used for a variety of purposes. In ancient civilizations, it was prized for its sharp edges, which made it ideal for crafting tools, weapons, and ceremonial objects. The Aztecs and Mayans used Obsidian mirrors for divination and scrying, believing that they could reveal hidden truths and provide glimpses into the future. Obsidian was also used in healing practices to remove blockages, draw out impurities, and promote emotional and spiritual healing.

One of the most notable properties of Obsidian is its association with transformation and change. It is a stone that encourages us to confront our shadow selves, release old patterns, and embrace personal growth. Obsidian acts as a mirror, reflecting back to us our deepest fears, limiting beliefs, and unresolved traumas. By facing these shadows, we can integrate them into our wholeness, heal emotional wounds, and transform our lives.

Obsidian is also a stone of truth. It helps us to see through illusions, pierce through deception, and uncover hidden truths about ourselves and the world around us. It encourages us to confront our own self-deception, challenge our assumptions, and seek authentic experiences. By working with Obsidian, we can gain a deeper understanding of our motivations, behaviors, and patterns, paving the way for greater self-awareness and personal growth.

Another key attribute of Obsidian is its protective qualities. It is believed to create a shield of energy around us, deflecting negativity and psychic attacks. Obsidian can also help to ground us, providing a sense of stability and security in the face of chaos and uncertainty. It is a stone that empowers us to set healthy boundaries, stand our ground, and protect our energy from those who would drain or manipulate us.

Obsidian is also a stone of release and purification. It helps us to let go of emotional baggage, toxic relationships, and self-limiting beliefs. By working with Obsidian, we can cut cords with the past, forgive ourselves and others, and move forward with a renewed sense of purpose and clarity. It is a powerful tool for those seeking to break free from unhealthy patterns, overcome addiction, and embrace a healthier, more fulfilling life.

In addition to its metaphysical properties, Obsidian is thought to have physical healing benefits. It is often used to relieve pain, reduce inflammation, and improve circulation. Obsidian is also said to support detoxification, strengthen the immune system, and aid in the healing of wounds and injuries. While scientific evidence for these claims is limited, the power of intention and the placebo effect can be significant in the healing process.

To harness the transformative energy of Obsidian, there are several ways to incorporate it into your daily life. Wearing Obsidian jewellery allows you to carry its protective and grounding energy with you wherever you go. Placing Obsidian in your home or workspace can create a more secure and energized environment. Meditating with Obsidian can help you to connect with your shadow self, release emotional blockages, and gain insights into your life purpose. You can also use Obsidian in crystal grids, scrying practices, or simply hold it in your hand while setting intentions for transformation, truth, and protection.

Obsidian, with its enigmatic beauty and powerful energy, is a true gift from the Earth. Its ability to shatter illusions, uncover truth, and facilitate profound personal transformation makes it an invaluable tool for those on a path of self-discovery, healing, and spiritual growth. Whether you're seeking to confront your shadow self, release emotional baggage, or simply gain a deeper understanding of yourself and the world around you, Obsidian is a powerful ally that can guide you on your journey towards greater authenticity, empowerment, and self-realization.

Remember, the true power of Obsidian lies not only in its inherent properties but also in your connection to its energy and your willingness to embrace its transformative potential. By approaching Obsidian with reverence, respect, and a willingness to confront your deepest truths, you can unlock its full potential and experience its profound impact on your life. So, let the obsidian mirror reflect back to you the hidden aspects of yourself, and let its transformative energy guide you towards a life of authenticity, empowerment, and spiritual awakening.

ppp

Obsidian, a mirror to the soul, shatters illusions and reveals the hidden truths within. Embrace its darkness, and emerge transformed with newfound clarity and strength.

ELEVEN

TURQUOISE: PROTECTION AND GOOD FORTUNE. SUBTITLE: ATTRACT LUCK AND BLESSINGS.

Turquoise, a captivating gemstone cherished for its striking blue-green hues, has been revered across cultures and civilizations for millennia as a talisman of protection, good fortune, and blessings. Its vibrant colours, reminiscent of clear skies and serene waters, evoke a sense of tranquility, wisdom, and spiritual connection. Let us embark on a journey through the fascinating world of Turquoise and explore how it can shield us from negativity, attract luck and blessings, and foster a deeper connection to our inner wisdom and the natural world.

The name "Turquoise" is believed to have originated from the French term "pierre turquoise," meaning "Turkish stone," as it was often traded through Turkey. This gemstone is a hydrous phosphate of copper and aluminum, formed through the interaction of mineral-rich water with surrounding rocks. Its distinct blue-green colour is attributed to the presence of copper, while varying amounts of iron can create greenish or yellowish hues. The unique patterns and matrix within Turquoise, often referred to as "spiderweb matrix," are formed by inclusions of other minerals, adding to its character and beauty.

Throughout history, Turquoise has held a special place in numerous cultures. Native American tribes in the southwestern United States considered Turquoise to be a sacred stone, believing it to be a gift from the sky and a symbol of protection, healing, and good fortune. It was often used in jewellery, ceremonial objects, and even inlayed into dwellings to ward off evil spirits and bring blessings to the home. In ancient Egypt, Turquoise was associated with the goddess Hathor, a symbol of joy, love, and motherhood. It was used in amulets and jewellery to protect against misfortune and attract good luck. Tibetan and Nepalese cultures also revered Turquoise, believing it to represent the sky and the earth, connecting the wearer to both the physical and spiritual realms.

One of the most prominent properties of Turquoise is its association with protection. It is believed to create a shield of positive energy around the wearer, deflecting negative energies and protecting against psychic attacks. This protective energy is thought to extend to both the physical and spiritual realms, shielding the wearer from accidents, illness, and misfortune. Turquoise is often worn as a talisman for protection while traveling, engaging in new ventures, or facing challenging situations.

Turquoise is also a stone of good fortune and blessings. It is believed to attract luck, abundance, and prosperity into one's life. In many cultures, Turquoise is considered a lucky charm, often given as a gift to wish someone well or to celebrate special occasions. It is thought to enhance creativity, attract opportunities, and open doors to new possibilities. By wearing or carrying Turquoise, one can invite positive energy, abundance, and good fortune into their life.

Another key attribute of Turquoise is its connection to wisdom and intuition. It is believed to enhance mental clarity, improve communication, and deepen one's connection to their inner wisdom. Turquoise is said to stimulate the throat chakra, the energy center associated with communication and self-expression, enabling one to speak their truth with confidence and clarity. It is also thought to activate the third eye chakra, the energy center associated with intuition and insight, allowing one to access their inner wisdom and receive guidance from higher realms.

Turquoise is also a stone of healing and balance. It is believed to have a calming effect on the emotions, promote tranquility, and alleviate stress and anxiety. It is said to help one to release negative emotions, forgive past hurts, and move forward with a renewed sense of peace and optimism. Turquoise is also thought to have physical healing properties, particularly for the respiratory and immune systems. It is often used to alleviate sore throats, allergies, and respiratory ailments, as well as to boost the immune system and promote overall well-being.

To harness the transformative energy of Turquoise, there are various ways to incorporate it into your daily life. Wearing Turquoise jewellery allows you to carry its protective and lucky energy with you wherever you go. Placing Turquoise in your home or workspace can create a more peaceful and positive environment. Meditating with Turquoise can deepen your connection to your inner wisdom, enhance your intuition, and promote emotional healing. You can also use Turquoise in crystal grids, elixirs, or simply hold it in your hand while setting intentions for protection, good fortune, and blessings.

Turquoise, with its vibrant hues and captivating energy, is a true gift from the Earth. Its ability to protect, bring good fortune, and enhance wisdom makes it an invaluable tool for personal growth, spiritual development, and overall well-being. Whether you are seeking protection from negativity, attracting luck and abundance, or deepening your connection to your inner wisdom and the natural world, Turquoise is a powerful ally that can guide you on your journey towards greater peace, prosperity, and fulfillment.

Remember, the true power of Turquoise lies not only in its inherent properties but also in your connection to its energy and your intention to harness its gifts. By approaching Turquoise with reverence, gratitude, and an open heart, you can unlock its full potential and experience its transformative effects on your life. So, let the vibrant energy of Turquoise envelop you in its protective embrace, guide you towards good fortune, and illuminate your path with wisdom and blessings.

ϼϼϼ

Turquoise, a talisman of protection and good fortune, shields us from negativity and attracts blessings into our lives. Adorn yourself with its vibrant blue, and walk your path with confidence and grace.

TWELVE
PERIDOT: HAPPINESS AND EMOTIONAL HEALING. SUBTITLE: LET GO OF NEGATIVITY.

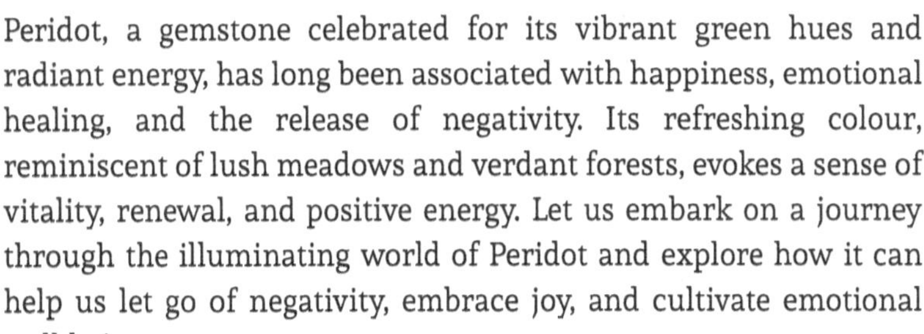

Peridot, a gemstone celebrated for its vibrant green hues and radiant energy, has long been associated with happiness, emotional healing, and the release of negativity. Its refreshing colour, reminiscent of lush meadows and verdant forests, evokes a sense of vitality, renewal, and positive energy. Let us embark on a journey through the illuminating world of Peridot and explore how it can help us let go of negativity, embrace joy, and cultivate emotional well-being.

The name "Peridot" is believed to have originated from the Arabic word "faridat," meaning "gem." This gemstone is one of the few that occur in only one colour, a vivid green that ranges from yellowish-green to olive green, depending on the amount of iron present in its crystal structure. This vibrant green colour is associated with the heart chakra, the energy center located in the center of the chest. The heart chakra governs our emotions, compassion, love, and sense of well-being. By working with Peridot, we can stimulate and balance this chakra, promoting emotional healing, fostering positive emotions, and letting go of negativity.

Peridot has a rich history intertwined with various cultures and traditions. In ancient Egypt, it was known as the "gem of the sun" and believed to be a gift from the sun god Ra. It was used in jewellery and amulets to protect against evil spirits, nightmares, and negative energies. The Egyptians also believed that Peridot could enhance confidence, courage, and personal power. In Hawaiian folklore, Peridot is associated with Pele, the goddess of fire and volcanoes. It is believed to be tears of Pele, symbolizing the transformative power of fire and the renewal that follows destruction. Throughout history, Peridot has been cherished as a stone of happiness, abundance, and spiritual growth.

One of the most remarkable properties of Peridot is its association with happiness and positive energy. Its vibrant green colour radiates joy, optimism, and a zest for life. By wearing or carrying Peridot, we can invite this positive energy into our lives, uplifting our spirits, and promoting a sense of well-being. Peridot is a stone that reminds us to focus on the good things in life, appreciate the present moment, and cultivate a joyful and optimistic outlook.

Peridot is also a powerful stone for emotional healing. It helps us to release past traumas, forgive ourselves and others, and let go of negative emotions such as anger, resentment, and jealousy. By working with Peridot, we can break free from patterns of self-sabotage, overcome emotional blockages, and cultivate healthier relationships with ourselves and others. It is a stone that encourages us to embrace our true selves, express our emotions authentically, and live a life filled with love, joy, and inner peace.

Another key attribute of Peridot is its ability to promote abundance and prosperity. It is believed to attract wealth, success, and good fortune into our lives. By working with Peridot, we can shift our mindset from scarcity to abundance, allowing us to see the unlimited possibilities that surround us. It encourages us to take action towards our goals, trust in the universe's abundance, and embrace the flow of prosperity into our lives.

Peridot is also a stone of protection and purification. It is believed to create a shield of positive energy around the wearer, deflecting negativity and harmful energies. It can also help to cleanse and purify the aura, removing any energetic blockages or imbalances. By working with Peridot, we can strengthen our energetic boundaries, protect ourselves from negative influences, and maintain a healthy and vibrant energy field.

In addition to its metaphysical properties, Peridot is thought to have physical healing benefits. It is often used to support the liver, gallbladder, and digestive system. Peridot is also said to alleviate stress, promote restful sleep, and enhance overall vitality. While scientific evidence for these claims is limited, the power of intention and the placebo effect can be significant in the healing process.

To harness the transformative energy of Peridot, there are many ways to incorporate it into your daily life. Wearing Peridot jewellery allows you to carry its joyful and healing energy with you wherever you go. Placing Peridot in your home or workspace can create a more positive and energized environment. Meditating with Peridot can help you to connect with your heart center, release emotional baggage, and cultivate a greater sense of happiness and well-being. You can also use Peridot in crystal grids, elixirs, or simply hold it in your hand while setting intentions for emotional healing, letting go of negativity, and embracing joy.

Peridot, with its vibrant green hues and radiant energy, is a true gem in the world of crystals. Its ability to promote happiness, emotional healing, and abundance makes it an invaluable tool for personal growth and well-being. Whether you are seeking to overcome negativity, heal emotional wounds, or simply invite more joy and abundance into your life, Peridot is a powerful ally that can guide you on your journey towards greater emotional well-being, happiness, and spiritual growth.

Remember, the true power of Peridot lies not only in its inherent properties but also in your connection to its energy and your willingness to embrace its joyful and healing vibrations. By approaching Peridot with an open heart and a positive mindset, you can unlock its full potential and experience its transformative effects on your emotional, mental, and physical well-being. So, let the radiant energy of Peridot illuminate your path, fill your heart with joy, and empower you to let go of negativity and embrace the abundance of life.

ҍҍҍ

Peridot, a beacon of joy and healing, dispels negativity and fills our hearts with light. Embrace its vibrant green, and let its energy wash over you, bringing happiness and emotional well-being.

THIRTEEN

FLUORITE: FOCUS AND CONCENTRATION. SUBTITLE: ENHANCE MENTAL CLARITY.

Fluorite, a mesmerizing gemstone celebrated for its vibrant and diverse range of colours, is a stone of focus, concentration, and mental clarity. Its captivating beauty and powerful metaphysical properties have made it a cherished tool for students, scholars, and anyone seeking to enhance their mental acuity and focus. Let us embark on a journey into the vibrant world of Fluorite and explore how it can sharpen our minds, improve concentration, and unlock our intellectual potential.

The name "Fluorite" is derived from the Latin word "fluere," meaning "to flow," referring to its ability to lower the melting point of other minerals. This gemstone is composed of calcium fluoride and is found in a variety of colours, including purple, green, blue, yellow, and even colourless varieties. Each colour is associated with different properties and benefits, but all share the common theme of enhancing mental clarity and focus. The cubic crystal structure of Fluorite is believed to represent stability, order, and mental organization, further emphasizing its connection to mental clarity and focus.

Fluorite has a long and rich history intertwined with various cultures and traditions. In ancient Rome, it was used in decorative objects and believed to possess protective qualities. The Chinese used Fluorite in carvings and sculptures, associating it with good fortune and prosperity. Medieval alchemists believed that Fluorite could transmute base metals into gold and used it in their experiments. Throughout history, Fluorite has been valued for its ability to enhance mental clarity, improve concentration, and promote spiritual growth.

One of the most remarkable properties of Fluorite is its ability to enhance focus and concentration. It is believed to clear the mind of distractions, improve memory, and facilitate deeper levels of concentration. By working with Fluorite, students can enhance their learning abilities, professionals can improve their productivity, and anyone can experience greater mental clarity and focus in their daily lives. Fluorite is often used in meditation and mindfulness practices to quiet the mind, enhance focus, and achieve a state of mental stillness.

Fluorite is also a stone of mental clarity and organization. It helps to bring order to chaotic thoughts, streamline mental processes, and improve decision-making abilities. By working with Fluorite, we can gain a clearer understanding of complex issues, break down problems into manageable steps, and approach challenges with a calm and focused mind. It is a valuable tool for anyone who struggles with information overload, mental clutter, or difficulty making decisions.

Another key attribute of Fluorite is its ability to stimulate creativity and innovation. It is believed to open the mind to new possibilities, enhance creative thinking, and inspire innovative solutions. By working with Fluorite, artists, writers, and other creative individuals can tap into their creative flow, overcome mental blocks, and generate new ideas. It is also a helpful tool for problem-solving, as it can help us to see things from a different perspective and find unique solutions to complex challenges.

Fluorite is also a stone of spiritual development and intuition. It is believed to enhance psychic abilities, connect us with our higher selves, and facilitate spiritual growth. By meditating with Fluorite, we can access higher realms of consciousness, receive divine guidance, and deepen our connection to the spiritual realm. It is also said to help us to understand and interpret our dreams, enhance our intuition, and develop our psychic gifts.

In addition to its metaphysical properties, Fluorite is thought to have physical healing benefits. It is often used to strengthen bones and teeth, support the immune system, and alleviate pain and inflammation. Fluorite is also said to improve coordination, balance, and physical dexterity. While scientific evidence for these claims is limited, the power of intention and the placebo effect can be significant in the healing process.

To harness the transformative energy of Fluorite, there are several ways to incorporate it into your daily life. Wearing Fluorite jewellery allows you to carry its focusing and clarifying energy with you wherever you go. Placing Fluorite in your home or workspace can create a more peaceful, productive, and mentally stimulating environment. Meditating with Fluorite can help you to quiet the mind, enhance focus, and access higher states of consciousness. You can also use Fluorite in crystal grids, elixirs, or simply hold it in your hand while setting intentions for mental clarity, focus, and creativity.

Fluorite, with its vibrant colours and powerful metaphysical properties, is a true gem in the world of crystals. Its ability to enhance mental clarity, improve concentration, and stimulate creativity makes it an invaluable tool for personal growth, intellectual development, and spiritual well-being. Whether you're a student seeking to improve your grades, a professional looking to enhance your productivity, or simply someone who wants to sharpen their mind and focus, Fluorite is a powerful ally that can support you on your journey towards greater mental clarity, focus, and intellectual achievement.

Remember, the true power of Fluorite lies not only in its inherent properties but also in your connection to its energy and your intention to harness its gifts. By approaching Fluorite with an open mind and a willingness to explore its depths, you can unlock its full potential and experience its transformative effects on your mind, body, and spirit. So, let the vibrant energy of Fluorite illuminate your mind, sharpen your focus, and guide you towards a life of greater clarity, creativity, and intellectual fulfillment.

ᚦᚦᚦ

Fluorite, a prism of mental clarity, sharpens our focus and unlocks our intellectual potential. Let its vibrant colours guide your thoughts, and experience a newfound clarity and concentration.

FOURTEEN

GARNET: PASSION AND REVITALIZATION. SUBTITLE: BOOST ENERGY AND STAMINA.

Garnet, a gemstone celebrated for its deep, rich red hues and fiery energy, has long been associated with passion, vitality, and revitalization. Its captivating beauty and powerful metaphysical properties have made it a cherished talisman for those seeking to ignite their passions, boost their energy levels, and enhance their overall stamina. Let us embark on a journey through the vibrant world of Garnet and explore how it can awaken our inner fire, revitalize our bodies and minds, and empower us to live life with passion and purpose.

The name "Garnet" is believed to derive from the Latin word

"granatum," meaning "pomegranate," due to the gemstone's resemblance to the vibrant red seeds of the fruit. Garnet is not a single mineral but a group of minerals with similar crystal structures and chemical compositions. The most common type of Garnet is Almandine, which is typically a deep red colour. However, Garnet can also be found in a variety of other colours, including green, orange, yellow, and even black. Each colour is associated with different properties and benefits, but all share the common theme of passion, energy, and revitalization.

Garnet has a rich and storied history that spans cultures and continents. In ancient Egypt, it was considered a symbol of life, energy, and power. Garnet jewellery was worn by pharaohs and royalty as a symbol of their status and authority. It was also believed to protect against evil spirits and bring good fortune. In Greek mythology, Garnet is associated with Hades, the god of the underworld, and Persephone, the goddess of spring. It is said to be a symbol of their love and the cycle of life, death, and rebirth. Throughout history, Garnet has been valued for its ability to revitalize the body and mind, stimulate passion and creativity, and enhance courage and strength.

One of the most notable properties of Garnet is its association with passion and vitality. It is a stone that ignites the fire within, awakening our desires, and inspiring us to pursue our passions with fervor. Garnet helps to overcome lethargy, apathy, and lack of motivation, empowering us to take action towards our goals and live life to the fullest. It is a stone that reminds us of our inner strength and encourages us to embrace our passions with unwavering enthusiasm.

Garnet is also a powerful stone for revitalization and rejuvenation. It is believed to stimulate the life force energy within us, known as "chi" or "prana," and promote overall well-being. Garnet can help to restore energy levels, enhance physical stamina, and improve circulation. It is a stone that can be particularly helpful for those who are feeling depleted, exhausted, or recovering from illness or injury. By working with Garnet, we can revitalize our bodies and minds, enhance our vitality, and experience a renewed sense of energy and enthusiasm for life.

Another key attribute of Garnet is its connection to courage and inner strength. It is a stone that empowers us to face our fears, overcome challenges, and persevere through difficult times. Garnet can help us to cultivate a sense of inner resilience, determination, and confidence. It is a stone that reminds us of our own power and encourages us to stand up for what we believe in, even in the face of adversity. Garnet can be particularly supportive for those who are going through major life transitions, facing difficult decisions, or struggling with self-doubt.

Garnet is also a stone of love and commitment. It is believed to enhance passion, intimacy, and devotion in relationships. Garnet can help to reignite the spark in long-term relationships, deepen emotional connections, and foster a sense of love and loyalty. It is a stone that can be particularly helpful for those who are seeking to attract new love, strengthen existing relationships, or heal from past heartbreaks.

In addition to its metaphysical properties, Garnet is thought to have physical healing benefits. It is often used to improve circulation, stimulate the metabolism, and support the immune system. Garnet is also said to aid in detoxification, purify the blood, and enhance overall vitality. While scientific evidence for these claims is limited, the power of intention and the placebo effect can be significant in the healing process.

To harness the transformative energy of Garnet, there are several ways to incorporate it into your daily life. Wearing Garnet jewellery allows you to carry its passionate and revitalizing energy with you wherever you go. Placing Garnet in your home or workspace can create a more energized and vibrant atmosphere. Meditating with Garnet can help you to connect with your inner fire, ignite your passions, and enhance your personal power. You can also use Garnet in crystal grids, elixirs, or simply hold it in your hand while setting intentions for passion, revitalization, and courage.

Garnet, with its fiery red hues and powerful energy, is a true gift from the Earth. Its ability to ignite passion, boost energy, and enhance stamina makes it an invaluable tool for personal growth, self-empowerment, and overall well-being. Whether you are seeking to revitalize your body and mind, overcome challenges, or simply live life with greater passion and purpose, Garnet is a powerful ally that can guide you on your journey towards greater vitality, courage, and fulfillment.

Remember, the true power of Garnet lies not only in its inherent properties but also in your connection to its energy and your willingness to embrace its passionate and revitalizing vibrations. By approaching Garnet with an open heart and a fiery spirit, you can unlock its full potential and experience its transformative effects on your physical, emotional, and spiritual well-being.

ᗞᗞᗞ

Garnet, a fiery ember of passion, ignites the flames of desire and revitalizes the soul. Embrace its warmth, and let its energy fuel your passions and drive you towards success.

FIFTEEN

ONYX: STRENGTH AND WILLPOWER. SUBTITLE: OVERCOME CHALLENGES WITH RESILIENCE.

Onyx, a striking gemstone renowned for its deep black colour and smooth texture, has long been revered as a symbol of strength, willpower, and resilience. Its enigmatic beauty and powerful metaphysical properties have drawn those seeking inner fortitude, protection, and the ability to overcome challenges to its depths for centuries. Let us embark on a journey into the empowering world of Onyx and explore how it can fortify our resolve, enhance our willpower, and help us navigate life's obstacles with grace and resilience.

The name "Onyx" is derived from the Greek word "onux," meaning "nail" or "claw," perhaps due to its resemblance to a fingernail when polished. Onyx is a variety of chalcedony, a cryptocrystalline form of quartz. Its characteristic black colour is attributed to the presence of impurities, such as carbon or iron oxide. Onyx can also occur in other colours, including white, brown, and banded varieties, but black Onyx is the most well-known and sought-after for its association with strength and protection.

Throughout history, Onyx has been valued for its protective qualities and its ability to enhance strength and willpower. In ancient Egypt, it was believed to ward off evil spirits and negative energies, and it was often used in amulets and talismans for protection. Roman soldiers wore Onyx jewellery for courage and strength in battle, while Greek warriors believed it could make them invincible. In the Middle Ages, Onyx was associated with Saturn, the planet of discipline, responsibility, and endurance. It was believed to enhance self-control, focus, and perseverance.

One of the most notable properties of Onyx is its association with strength and willpower. It is a stone that empowers us to face challenges with courage, overcome obstacles with determination, and persevere through difficult times. Onyx helps us to tap into our inner strength, bolster our resolve, and stay focused on our goals. By working with Onyx, we can develop the mental and emotional fortitude needed to overcome adversity, resist temptation, and achieve our dreams.

Onyx is also a stone of protection and grounding. It is believed to create a shield of positive energy around us, deflecting negativity and harmful influences. Onyx can also help to ground us in the present moment, providing a sense of stability and security in the face of chaos and uncertainty. It is a stone that empowers us to set healthy boundaries, stand our ground, and protect our energy from those who would drain or manipulate us.

Another key attribute of Onyx is its ability to enhance self-discipline and focus. It is a stone that helps us to stay on track, resist distractions, and achieve our goals. Onyx can be particularly helpful for those who struggle with procrastination, lack of motivation, or difficulty staying focused on tasks. By working with Onyx, we can develop the self-discipline and mental clarity needed to overcome these challenges and achieve success.

Onyx is also a stone of emotional healing and release. It is believed to absorb negative energies and emotions, helping us to let go of past traumas, grief, and anger. Onyx can also help to soothe anxiety, calm the mind, and promote emotional balance. By working with Onyx, we can process difficult emotions, release emotional blockages, and move forward with a renewed sense of inner peace and well-being.

In addition to its metaphysical properties, Onyx is thought to have physical healing benefits. It is often used to strengthen bones and teeth, improve circulation, and support the immune system. Onyx is also said to alleviate pain, reduce inflammation, and aid in the healing of wounds and injuries. While scientific evidence for these claims is limited, the power of intention and the placebo effect can be significant in the healing process.

To harness the transformative energy of Onyx, there are several ways to incorporate it into your daily life. Wearing Onyx jewellery allows you to carry its protective and empowering energy with you wherever you go. Placing Onyx in your home or workspace can create a more grounded, focused, and energized environment. Meditating with Onyx can help you to connect with your inner strength, release negative emotions, and enhance your willpower. You can also use Onyx in crystal grids, elixirs, or simply hold it in your hand while setting intentions for strength, resilience, and overcoming challenges.

Onyx, with its deep black colour and powerful energy, is a true gift from the Earth. Its ability to enhance strength, willpower, and resilience makes it an invaluable tool for personal growth, self-empowerment, and overcoming life's obstacles. Whether you are facing a difficult situation, seeking to develop greater self-discipline, or simply want to feel more grounded and empowered, Onyx is a powerful ally that can support you on your journey towards greater strength, resilience, and inner peace.

Remember, the true power of Onyx lies not only in its inherent properties but also in your connection to its energy and your willingness to embrace its transformative potential. By approaching Onyx with respect, intention, and an open heart, you can unlock its full potential and experience its profound impact on your life. So, let the deep black energy of Onyx fortify your resolve, strengthen your willpower, and guide you towards a life of greater resilience, courage, and unwavering inner strength.

 PPP

Onyx, a pillar of strength and willpower, empowers us to overcome challenges and persevere with unwavering determination. With its unwavering support, we can face any obstacle and emerge victorious.

SIXTEEN

Aquamarine: Calmness and Tranquility. Subtitle: Find inner peace and clarity.

Aquamarine, a gemstone of serene blues and greens, evokes the tranquility of the ocean and the clarity of the sky. With its soothing energy and calming vibrations, Aquamarine has long been revered as a stone of peace, tranquility, and emotional healing. Let us delve into the depths of this captivating gem and discover how it can help us find inner peace, enhance communication, and navigate the waters of life with grace and serenity.

The name "Aquamarine" originates from the Latin words "aqua" (water) and "marina" (of the sea), aptly describing its mesmerizing blue-green colour. Aquamarine is a variety of beryl, a mineral family that also includes emerald. Its colour is caused by trace amounts of iron within its crystal structure. The intensity of the blue can vary, ranging from pale to deep blue, often with a hint of green. Aquamarine's clarity and transparency further enhance its association with water, reflecting the clarity of mind and emotional calmness it is believed to promote.

Aquamarine has a rich history intertwined with various cultures and traditions. Ancient mariners believed that Aquamarine was a treasure from mermaids and wore it as a talisman for protection and safe passage at sea. In ancient Rome, Aquamarine was associated with Neptune, the god of the sea, and was believed to bring good fortune to sailors and travelers. It was also used in love charms and amulets to promote marital happiness and fidelity. In the Middle Ages, Aquamarine was thought to have the power to reveal the truth and protect against poison. Throughout history, Aquamarine has been cherished as a stone of peace, tranquility, and emotional healing.

One of the most remarkable properties of Aquamarine is its association with calmness and tranquility. Its soothing energy helps to alleviate stress, anxiety, and emotional turmoil. By working with Aquamarine, we can find inner peace, balance our emotions, and navigate life's challenges with greater ease and serenity. Aquamarine is often used in meditation and relaxation practices to quiet the mind, reduce mental chatter, and induce a state of deep tranquility. Its calming vibrations can also help to soothe frayed nerves, promote restful sleep, and reduce feelings of overwhelm.

Aquamarine is also a stone of communication and self-expression. It encourages us to speak our truth with clarity, compassion, and confidence. It helps us to articulate our thoughts and feelings effectively, express our needs and desires, and communicate our boundaries with assertiveness and grace. By working with Aquamarine, we can improve our communication skills, enhance our relationships, and foster greater understanding and harmony in our interactions with others.

Another key attribute of Aquamarine is its ability to promote emotional healing and release. It helps us to let go of past traumas, forgive ourselves and others, and release negative emotions such as anger, resentment, and grief. Aquamarine's soothing energy creates a safe space for emotional processing, allowing us to explore our feelings, understand their origins, and release them in a healthy and constructive way. It is a powerful tool for those seeking to heal emotional wounds, cultivate emotional resilience, and develop a deeper connection to their inner wisdom.

Aquamarine is also a stone of intuition and spiritual awareness. It is believed to enhance our psychic abilities, connect us with our higher selves, and deepen our spiritual connection. By meditating with Aquamarine, we can access higher realms of consciousness, receive divine guidance, and gain insights into our life purpose. It is also said to help us to interpret our dreams, develop our intuition, and connect with our spirit guides.

In addition to its metaphysical properties, Aquamarine is thought to have physical healing benefits. It is often used to soothe sore throats, alleviate respiratory ailments, and boost the immune system. Aquamarine is also said to support thyroid health, regulate hormones, and reduce inflammation. While scientific evidence for these claims is limited, the power of intention and the placebo effect can be significant in the healing process.

To harness the transformative energy of Aquamarine, there are several ways to incorporate it into your daily life. Wearing Aquamarine jewellery allows you to carry its calming and peaceful energy with you wherever you go. Placing Aquamarine in your home or workspace can create a more serene and harmonious environment. Meditating with Aquamarine can help you to quiet the mind, release stress and anxiety, and connect with your inner peace. You can also use Aquamarine in crystal grids, elixirs, or simply hold it in your hand while setting intentions for calmness, tranquility, and emotional healing.

Aquamarine, with its serene beauty and gentle energy, is a true gift from the Earth. Its ability to promote calmness, tranquility, and emotional healing makes it an invaluable tool for personal growth, spiritual development, and overall well-being. Whether you are seeking to reduce stress, improve communication, or simply find more peace and serenity in your life, Aquamarine is a powerful ally that can guide you on your journey towards greater emotional balance, inner peace, and spiritual awakening.

Remember, the true power of Aquamarine lies not only in its inherent properties but also in your connection to its energy and your intention to harness its gifts. By approaching Aquamarine with an open heart and a willingness to surrender to its calming embrace, you can unlock its full potential and experience its transformative effects on your emotional, mental, and physical well-being. So, let the serene energy of Aquamarine wash over you, calming your mind, soothing your emotions, and guiding you towards a life filled with inner peace, clarity, and tranquility.

ᗐᗐᗐ

Aquamarine, a tranquil oasis of peace, soothes the soul and brings calmness to the mind. Submerge yourself in its serene waters, and find solace in its tranquil embrace.

SEVENTEEN

JADE: HARMONY AND BALANCE. SUBTITLE: ATTRACT GOOD LUCK AND PROSPERITY.

Jade, a gemstone revered for its exquisite green hue and profound metaphysical properties, has been cherished for centuries as a symbol of harmony, balance, and good fortune. Its captivating beauty and powerful energy have inspired artists, philosophers, and spiritual seekers to seek its guidance and embrace its transformative potential. Let us embark on a journey through the rich history and symbolism of Jade, exploring how it can bring harmony and balance to our lives, attract good luck and prosperity, and foster a deeper connection to our inner wisdom and the natural world.

The name "Jade" is derived from the Spanish term "piedra de ijada," meaning "stone of the side," referring to its purported ability to heal ailments of the kidneys and loins. However, Jade is not a single mineral but rather a collective term for two distinct minerals: Nephrite and Jadeite. Nephrite is the most common form of Jade and is known for its toughness and durability. Jadeite, on the other hand, is rarer and more valuable, often prized for its vibrant green colour and translucency. Both forms of Jade share similar metaphysical properties and have been revered for their beauty and spiritual significance throughout history.

Jade holds a prominent place in various cultures and civilizations. In ancient China, it was considered the "imperial gem" and was highly valued for its beauty, durability, and association with virtue, wisdom, and prosperity. Jade was carved into intricate ornaments, ritual objects, and even burial suits for royalty, symbolizing their status and connection to the divine. In Maori culture, Jade, known as "pounamu," is considered a sacred treasure and a symbol of identity, strength, and connection to ancestors. It is used in carvings, weapons, and jewellery, each piece imbued with cultural significance and spiritual meaning. Central American civilizations, such as the Maya and Olmec, also revered Jade, crafting intricate masks, figurines, and adornments from this precious stone.

One of the most profound qualities of Jade is its association with harmony and balance. It is believed to promote emotional balance, inner peace, and a sense of serenity. By working with Jade, we can harmonize our emotions, find equilibrium in our lives, and cultivate a greater sense of inner peace. Jade is also said to balance the yin and yang energies within us, promoting a harmonious flow of energy throughout the body and mind. This balance can manifest in improved physical health, emotional well-being, and a greater sense of overall harmony in our lives.

Jade is also a stone of good luck and prosperity. It is believed to attract abundance, success, and good fortune into our lives. In many cultures, Jade is considered a lucky charm, often given as a gift to wish someone well or to celebrate special occasions. It is thought to enhance our ability to manifest our desires, attract opportunities, and achieve our goals. By wearing or carrying Jade, we can invite positive energy, abundance, and good fortune into our lives.

Another key attribute of Jade is its connection to wisdom and intuition. It is believed to enhance our mental clarity, improve our decision-making abilities, and deepen our connection to our inner wisdom. Jade is said to stimulate the heart chakra, the energy center associated with love, compassion, and emotional well-being, allowing us to approach life's challenges with greater understanding and empathy. It is also thought to activate the third eye chakra, the energy center associated with intuition and insight, helping us to trust our gut feelings and make decisions that are aligned with our highest good.

Jade is also a stone of protection and healing. It is believed to create a shield of positive energy around the wearer, protecting against negative energies and harmful influences. Jade is also said to have physical healing properties, particularly for the kidneys, liver, and spleen. It is often used to detoxify the body, strengthen the immune system, and promote overall health and well-being. While scientific evidence for these claims is limited, the power of intention and the placebo effect can be significant in the healing process.

To harness the transformative energy of Jade, there are several ways to incorporate it into your daily life. Wearing Jade jewellery allows you to carry its harmonious and protective energy with you wherever you go. Placing Jade in your home or workspace can create a more peaceful, balanced, and prosperous environment. Meditating with Jade can help you to connect with your inner wisdom, find emotional balance, and attract abundance into your life. You can also use Jade in crystal grids, elixirs, or simply hold it in your hand while setting intentions for harmony, balance, and good fortune.

Jade, with its exquisite beauty and profound metaphysical properties, is a true gift from the Earth. Its ability to bring harmony and balance to our lives, attract good luck and prosperity, and enhance our wisdom makes it an invaluable tool for personal growth, spiritual development, and overall well-being. Whether you are seeking to find inner peace, attract abundance, or deepen your connection to your inner wisdom and the natural world, Jade is a powerful ally that can guide you on your journey towards greater harmony, balance, and fulfillment in life.

Remember, the true power of Jade lies not only in its inherent properties but also in your connection to its energy and your intention to harness its gifts. By approaching Jade with reverence, gratitude, and an open heart, you can unlock its full potential and experience its transformative effects on your life. So, let the serene energy of Jade envelop you in its harmonious embrace, guide you towards a life of balance and prosperity, and awaken your inner wisdom to its fullest potential.

ppp

Jade, a harmonious symphony of green, balances our energies and attracts abundance into our lives. Hold its smooth touch, and let its energy guide you towards prosperity and well-being.

EIGHTEEN

SUNSTONE: LEADERSHIP AND SELF-CONFIDENCE. SUBTITLE: SHINE YOUR LIGHT.

Sunstone, a radiant gemstone shimmering with golden light, has long been revered as a stone of leadership, self-confidence, and personal power. Its warm and invigorating energy evokes the life-giving warmth of the sun, inspiring us to embrace our individuality, shine our light, and step into our true potential. Let us embark on a journey through the illuminating world of Sunstone and discover how it can ignite our inner fire, empower us to lead with confidence, and radiate our unique gifts out into the world.

The name "Sunstone" aptly reflects its association with the sun, the celestial body that sustains life and provides warmth, light, and energy. Sunstone's captivating shimmer is caused by tiny metallic inclusions, often composed of hematite or goethite, which reflect light and create a sparkling effect known as aventurescence. The colour of Sunstone can range from warm orange and red to shimmering gold and even green, each with its unique energy and symbolism.

Sunstone holds a rich history intertwined with various cultures and spiritual traditions. In ancient Greece, it was associated with the god Helios, the personification of the sun, and was believed to bring strength, vitality, and good fortune. Viking seafarers are said to have used Sunstone as a navigational tool, utilizing its light-reflecting properties to determine the position of the sun even on cloudy days. Native American tribes revered Sunstone as a sacred stone, believing it to connect them to the spiritual realm and enhance their connection to the natural world. Throughout history, Sunstone has been cherished as a talisman for leadership, personal power, and spiritual enlightenment.

One of the most profound qualities of Sunstone is its association with leadership and personal power. It is a stone that empowers us to step into our authentic selves, embrace our unique gifts, and lead with confidence and charisma. Sunstone helps us to overcome self-doubt, fear of failure, and the need for external validation, allowing us to trust in our own abilities and step into our rightful place as leaders in our lives and communities. By working with Sunstone, we can cultivate a strong sense of self-worth, develop our leadership skills, and inspire others with our vision and passion.

Sunstone is also a stone of self-confidence and empowerment. It helps us to recognize our own strengths, embrace our individuality, and shine our light in the world. Sunstone can help us to overcome shyness, insecurity, and fear of judgment, allowing us to express ourselves authentically and confidently. It is a stone that encourages us to celebrate our unique gifts, embrace our differences, and step into our personal power. By working with Sunstone, we can cultivate a radiant self-confidence that attracts positive energy, opportunities, and relationships into our lives.

Another key attribute of Sunstone is its connection to joy, optimism, and positive energy. Its warm and invigorating energy uplifts our spirits, dispels negativity, and promotes a sense of enthusiasm and zest for life. By working with Sunstone, we can cultivate a more positive outlook on life, attract joyful experiences, and create a ripple effect of positivity in the world around us. Sunstone is also believed to enhance creativity, inspire new ideas, and motivate us to take action towards our goals. It is a powerful tool for artists, entrepreneurs, and anyone who seeks to live a more vibrant and fulfilling life.

Sunstone is also a stone of vitality and physical energy. It is believed to stimulate the metabolism, boost energy levels, and enhance physical stamina. Sunstone is said to support the endocrine system, promote healthy digestion, and strengthen the immune system. While scientific evidence for these claims is limited, the power of intention and the placebo effect can be significant in the healing process.

To harness the transformative energy of Sunstone, there are several ways to incorporate it into your daily life. Wearing Sunstone jewellery allows you to carry its radiant energy with you wherever you go. Placing Sunstone in your home or workspace can create a more positive, energized, and inspiring environment. Meditating with Sunstone can help you to connect with your inner power, visualize your goals, and radiate your unique light. You can also use Sunstone in crystal grids, elixirs, or simply hold it in your hand while setting intentions for leadership, self-confidence, and personal empowerment.

Sunstone, with its radiant energy and shimmering beauty, is a true gift from the Earth. Its ability to ignite our inner fire, empower us to lead with confidence, and radiate our unique gifts makes it an invaluable tool for personal growth, self-discovery, and spiritual awakening. Whether you are seeking to step into your leadership potential, overcome self-doubt, or simply want to live a more joyful and fulfilling life, Sunstone is a powerful ally that can guide you on your journey towards greater self-confidence, personal power, and radiant self-expression.

Remember, the true power of Sunstone lies not only in its inherent properties but also in your connection to its energy and your willingness to embrace its radiant light. By approaching Sunstone with an open heart, a positive mindset, and a willingness to shine your light, you can unlock its full potential and experience its transformative effects on your life. So, let the warm and invigorating energy of Sunstone awaken your inner fire, empower you to lead with confidence, and illuminate your path towards a life filled with joy, purpose, and radiant self-expression.

Sunstone, a radiant sunbeam of confidence, empowers us to shine our light and lead with passion. Bask in its golden glow, and step into your personal power with grace and determination.

NINETEEN

OPAL: HOPE AND INSPIRATION. SUBTITLE: EMBRACE CREATIVITY AND IMAGINATION.

Opal, a mesmerizing gemstone renowned for its iridescent play of colour, has long been cherished as a stone of hope, inspiration, and creativity. Its captivating beauty and mystical properties have inspired artists, poets, and dreamers throughout the ages, drawing them into a world of wonder, imagination, and endless possibilities. Let us embark on a journey through the enchanting realm of Opal and explore how it can ignite our creativity, inspire our imaginations, and illuminate our path with hope and optimism.

The name "Opal" is believed to have originated from the Sanskrit word "upala," meaning "precious stone." Opals are formed from silica-rich solutions that seep into cracks and voids in rocks. Over time, the silica spheres within these solutions solidify and arrange themselves in a tightly packed pattern, creating the unique internal structure that gives Opal its characteristic play of colour, known as opalescence. This mesmerizing display of colours, ranging from fiery reds and oranges to calming blues and greens, has captivated humanity for centuries, inspiring awe and wonder at the beauty of nature's creations.

Throughout history, Opal has been associated with a myriad of beliefs and symbolism. In ancient Greece, it was believed to be a gift from the gods, granting the wearer foresight, protection, and the ability to understand dreams. The Romans considered Opal to be a symbol of hope, purity, and love, often using it in jewellery and amulets to attract good fortune and protect against evil spirits. In Aboriginal Australian culture, Opal is known as the "Rainbow Serpent" and is associated with creation, healing, and the spirit world. Throughout the ages, Opal has been cherished for its ability to inspire creativity, enhance imagination, and bring hope and optimism to those who wear it.

One of the most remarkable properties of Opal is its association with hope and inspiration. Its vibrant play of colour, reminiscent of rainbows and shimmering light, evokes a sense of wonder, joy, and optimism. By working with Opal, we can tap into our inner childlike wonder, rekindle our sense of hope, and find inspiration in the beauty and magic of the world around us. Opal can help us to see the possibilities that lie ahead, even in the face of adversity, and inspire us to pursue our dreams with renewed passion and enthusiasm.

Opal is also a stone of creativity and imagination. Its iridescent colours and shifting patterns stimulate our creative energies, encouraging us to think outside the box, explore new ideas, and express ourselves authentically. Opal is a powerful tool for artists, writers, musicians, and anyone who seeks to tap into their creative potential and bring their visions to life. By working with Opal, we can overcome creative blocks, enhance our imagination, and find new and innovative ways to express ourselves.

Another key attribute of Opal is its connection to emotional healing and self-awareness. It is believed to amplify our emotions, allowing us to process them in a healthy and constructive way. Opal can help us to identify and release emotional blockages, heal past traumas, and develop a deeper understanding of our emotional needs. It is also said to enhance our intuition, allowing us to tap into our inner wisdom and make decisions that are aligned with our highest good.

Opal is also a stone of love and passion. It is believed to enhance our capacity for love, deepen our emotional connections with others, and attract loving relationships into our lives. Opal can also help to rekindle passion and romance in existing relationships, promoting intimacy, communication, and mutual understanding. By working with Opal, we can open our hearts to love, attract loving relationships, and cultivate deeper connections with those we cherish.

In addition to its metaphysical properties, Opal is thought to have physical healing benefits. It is often used to strengthen the immune system, detoxify the body, and alleviate pain and inflammation. Opal is also said to support eye health, improve sleep, and enhance overall vitality. While scientific evidence for these claims is limited, the power of intention and the placebo effect can be significant in the healing process.

To harness the transformative energy of Opal, there are several ways to incorporate it into your daily life. Wearing Opal jewellery allows you to carry its inspiring and uplifting energy with you wherever you go. Placing Opal in your home or workspace can create a more creative, harmonious, and inspiring environment. Meditating with Opal can help you to connect with your inner child, awaken your creativity, and tap into your intuition. You can also use

Opal in crystal grids, elixirs, or simply hold it in your hand while setting intentions for hope, inspiration, and creative expression.

Opal, with its mesmerizing play of colour and mystical properties, is a true treasure from the Earth. Its ability to inspire hope, ignite creativity, and promote emotional healing makes it an invaluable tool for personal growth, self-expression, and spiritual development. Whether you are an artist seeking inspiration, a dreamer yearning to bring your visions to life, or simply someone who wants to live a more vibrant and fulfilling life, Opal is a powerful ally that can guide you on your journey towards greater creativity, imagination, and a life filled with hope and optimism.

Remember, the true power of Opal lies not only in its inherent properties but also in your connection to its energy and your willingness to embrace its transformative potential. By approaching Opal with an open heart, a playful spirit, and a thirst for inspiration, you can unlock its full potential and experience its profound impact on your creative expression, emotional well-being, and spiritual growth. So, let the shimmering colours of Opal illuminate your path, ignite your imagination, and guide you towards a life filled with hope, inspiration, and creative expression.

Opal, a kaleidoscope of dreams and inspiration, ignites our creativity and fuels our imagination. Embrace its iridescent play of colour, and let its magic guide you towards a life of wonder and possibility.

TWENTY

RUBY: LOVE AND PASSION. SUBTITLE: IGNITE THE FLAMES OF DESIRE.

Ruby, a gemstone of fiery red hues and intense vibrancy, has long been revered as a symbol of love, passion, and vitality. Its captivating beauty and powerful metaphysical properties have made it a cherished talisman for those seeking to ignite the flames of desire, deepen their relationships, and embrace life with unwavering passion. Let us embark on a journey through the enchanting world of Ruby and explore how it can awaken our hearts, ignite our passions, and empower us to live a life filled with love, joy, and vitality.

The name "Ruby" originates from the Latin word "ruber," meaning "red." This aptly describes its most striking feature: its deep, rich red colour, which has captured the imagination of cultures across the globe for centuries. Ruby is a variety of corundum, the second hardest mineral after diamond. Its red colour is caused by trace amounts of chromium, which also gives it its characteristic fluorescence. The intensity of the red can vary, ranging from a delicate pink to a deep, blood-red, with the most prized rubies exhibiting a vibrant pigeon blood red hue.

Ruby has a long and illustrious history intertwined with royalty, romance, and spiritual traditions. In ancient India, it was known as the "king of precious stones" and believed to be a source of protection, wealth, and good fortune. Rubies were often set in the crowns and jewellery of monarchs, symbolizing their power and authority. In Hinduism, Ruby is associated with the sun god Surya, representing vitality, energy, and the life force. In medieval Europe, Ruby was believed to protect against evil spirits, disease, and misfortune. It was also associated with love, passion, and fidelity, often given as a token of love and commitment.

One of the most remarkable properties of Ruby is its association with love and passion. It is a stone that ignites the fire within, awakening our desires, and inspiring us to pursue our passions with fervor. Ruby enhances our romantic relationships, deepening our emotional connection and fostering a sense of intimacy and passion. It is a stone that can help to rekindle the spark in long-term relationships, reignite the flames of desire, and bring back the excitement and passion that may have faded over time.

Ruby is also a stone of vitality and energy. It is believed to stimulate the life force energy within us, known as "chi" or "prana," and promote overall well-being. Ruby can help to boost our energy levels, enhance our physical stamina, and improve our circulation. It is a stone that can be particularly helpful for those who are feeling fatigued, lethargic, or lacking in motivation. By working with Ruby, we can revitalize our bodies and minds, enhance our physical and emotional vitality, and live life with greater passion and enthusiasm.

Another key attribute of Ruby is its connection to courage and self-confidence. It is a stone that empowers us to face our fears, overcome challenges, and step into our personal power. Ruby helps us to develop a strong sense of self-worth, believe in our abilities, and take risks to achieve our goals. It is a stone that encourages us to speak our truth, stand up for what we believe in, and live life with integrity and authenticity. By working with Ruby, we can cultivate a fearless spirit, embrace our true potential, and live life to the fullest.

Ruby is also a stone of protection and spiritual awareness. It is believed to shield us from negative energies, psychic attacks, and harmful influences. Ruby can also help to ground us in the present moment, connect us with our intuition, and enhance our spiritual connection. It is a stone that can be particularly helpful for those who are sensitive to energy or who work in environments where they are exposed to negativity.

In addition to its metaphysical properties, Ruby is thought to have physical healing benefits. It is often used to improve circulation, boost the immune system, and enhance vitality. Ruby is also said to support heart health, detoxify the body, and promote restful sleep. While scientific evidence for these claims is limited, the power of intention and the placebo effect can be significant in the healing process.

To harness the transformative energy of Ruby, there are several ways to incorporate it into your daily life. Wearing Ruby jewellery allows you to carry its passionate and revitalizing energy with you wherever you go. Placing Ruby in your home or bedroom can create a more passionate and energized atmosphere. Meditating with Ruby can help you to connect with your inner fire, ignite your passions, and enhance your personal power. You can also use Ruby in crystal grids, elixirs, or simply hold it in your hand while setting intentions for love, passion, and vitality.

Ruby, with its fiery red hues and captivating energy, is a true gift from the Earth. Its ability to ignite passion, boost energy, and enhance courage makes it an invaluable tool for personal growth, self-empowerment, and living a life filled with love, joy, and vitality. Whether you are seeking to deepen your relationships, revitalize your body and mind, or simply embrace life with greater passion and purpose, Ruby is a powerful ally that can guide you on your journey towards greater love, vitality, and fulfillment.

Remember, the true power of Ruby lies not only in its inherent properties but also in your connection to its energy and your willingness to embrace its passionate and revitalizing vibrations. By approaching Ruby with an open heart and a fiery spirit, you can unlock its full potential and experience its transformative effects on your physical, emotional, and spiritual well-being. So, let the radiant energy of Ruby ignite your passions, awaken your heart, and empower you to live life to the fullest with love, joy, and unwavering enthusiasm.

ϷϷϷ

Ruby, a fiery blaze of love and passion, awakens the heart and inspires us to live life to the fullest. Embrace its crimson embrace, and let its energy ignite the flames of desire within you.

TWENTY-ONE
SUMMARY

In the enchanting world of gemstones, each crystal holds a unique energy and purpose, offering us a pathway to healing, transformation, and self-discovery. Throughout history, cultures across the globe have revered these precious stones for their beauty, metaphysical properties, and ability to enhance our well-being. Let us embark on a journey through the shimmering landscape of crystals, exploring their diverse properties and the profound ways they can enrich our lives.

We begin with Amethyst, the stone of serenity, whose tranquil violet hues promote inner peace, intuition, and spiritual connection. It is a gemstone that calms the mind, soothes the emotions, and guides us towards a deeper understanding of ourselves and the universe. Rose Quartz, the stone of unconditional love, opens our hearts to compassion, forgiveness, and the boundless possibilities of love in all its forms. Its gentle pink energy nurtures emotional healing, promotes healthy relationships, and reminds us of our inherent worthiness of love.

Clear Quartz, the master healer, amplifies energy, promotes clarity, and purifies our energy field. Its pristine clarity symbolizes purity of thought and intention, making it a versatile tool for healing, manifestation, and spiritual growth. Citrine, the stone of abundance and prosperity, attracts joy, success, and positive energy into our lives. Its vibrant yellow hues ignite our inner light, inspire creativity, and empower us to manifest our desires.

Tiger's Eye, the stone of grounding and protection, strengthens our resolve, enhances our courage, and keeps us rooted in the present moment. Its shimmering golden-brown bands evoke the strength and resilience of a tiger, empowering us to face challenges with unwavering determination. Sodalite, the stone of communication and truth, encourages authentic self-expression, enhances intuition, and promotes harmonious communication with others. Its deep blue hues awaken our inner vision, enabling us to speak our truth with confidence and clarity.

Carnelian, the stone of creativity and vitality, ignites our passions, fuels our motivation, and unleashes our creative potential. Its fiery energy invigorates our bodies and minds, inspiring us to embrace our zest for life and pursue our dreams with renewed vigor. Moonstone, the stone of feminine energy and new beginnings, embraces the cyclical nature of life, promoting emotional balance, intuition, and a connection to the divine feminine. Its ethereal glow illuminates our path, guiding us through transitions and new beginnings with grace and serenity.

Lapis Lazuli, the stone of wisdom and self-expression, awakens our inner vision, enhances our communication, and unlocks the wisdom that resides within. Its deep blue colour, speckled with golden pyrite, evokes the vastness of the night sky and the wisdom of the cosmos. Obsidian, the stone of transformation and release, shatters illusions, uncovers hidden truths, and facilitates profound personal growth. Its dark, reflective surface acts as a mirror, revealing our shadows and guiding us towards greater self-awareness and healing.

Turquoise, the stone of protection and good fortune, shields us from negativity, attracts luck and blessings, and fosters a deeper connection to our inner wisdom and the natural world. Its vibrant blue-green hues evoke the tranquility of the ocean and the clarity of the sky, bringing us a sense of peace, protection, and spiritual connection. Peridot, the stone of happiness and emotional healing, promotes joy, optimism, and the release of negativity. Its vibrant green colour radiates positive energy, reminding us to appreciate the present moment and embrace life's blessings.

Fluorite, the stone of focus and concentration, enhances mental clarity, improves concentration, and stimulates creativity. Its diverse range of colours represents the spectrum of mental and emotional states, offering support for various aspects of our intellectual and creative pursuits. Garnet, the stone of passion and revitalization, ignites our inner fire, boosts our energy and stamina, and empowers us to live life with passion and purpose. Its fiery red hues awaken our desires, enhance our vitality, and inspire us to pursue our dreams with unwavering enthusiasm.

Onyx, the stone of strength and willpower, fortifies our resolve, enhances our resilience, and helps us to overcome challenges with grace and determination. Its deep black colour symbolizes strength, protection, and the ability to persevere through adversity. Aquamarine, the stone of calmness and tranquility, soothes our emotions, promotes inner peace, and enhances communication. Its serene blue-green hues evoke the tranquility of the ocean, bringing us a sense of calmness, clarity, and emotional balance.

Jade, the stone of harmony and balance, attracts good luck and prosperity, promotes emotional well-being, and enhances our connection to our inner wisdom. Its smooth texture and soothing green colour bring a sense of peace, balance, and harmony to our lives. Sunstone, the stone of leadership and self-confidence, empowers us to shine our light, embrace our individuality, and step into our true potential. Its radiant energy inspires confidence, optimism, and the courage to lead with passion and purpose.

Finally, Opal, the stone of hope and inspiration, embraces creativity and imagination, promoting emotional healing and self-awareness. Its iridescent play of colour sparks our imagination, encourages creative expression, and reminds us of the beauty and magic that surrounds us.

In conclusion, each gemstone in this enchanting collection offers unique gifts and insights, guiding us on a journey of self-discovery, healing, and transformation. By embracing the power of crystals, we can enhance our well-being, unlock our potential, and live a life filled with joy, abundance, and spiritual fulfillment. Whether you are drawn to the calming energy of Aquamarine, the fiery passion of Ruby, or the transformative power of Obsidian, these gemstones serve as powerful allies, supporting us on our individual paths towards greater self-awareness, healing, and empowerment. So, let the magic of crystals illuminate your life, and may their vibrant energies guide you towards a brighter, more fulfilling future.

ᐯᐯᐯ

Citation And References

This book represents the culmination of extensive research and meticulous analysis, incorporating a diverse range of sources, including numerous books, scholarly studies, and personal experiences. Additionally, I have scoured various websites to gather relevant information and data essential for the compilation of this work. I have taken every precaution to ensure the accuracy of the information presented and have diligently cited all sources to acknowledge their contributions.

Despite these efforts, the possibility of inadvertent errors remains. I deeply value the insights of my readers and appreciate any feedback that can help identify and rectify such inaccuracies. I encourage you to bring any discrepancies to my attention.

Your feedback is not only welcome but crucial, as it will aid in correcting current editions and enhancing the content of future ones. I am committed to maintaining the highest standards of accuracy and reliability in my work and thank you for your support and understanding.

Additionally, I firmly uphold the principle of freedom of speech and expression as guaranteed under Article 19(1)(a) of the Constitution of India, and I respect the diverse viewpoints and expressions of all readers.

ΡΡΡ

Other Books Of The Author

1. Empowering Minds: A Journey into Women's Self-Discovery and Power
2. The Dynamics of Motivation: Catalyzing Thought into Action
3. Meditation and Mental Well Being: The Path to Inner Peace and Clarity
4. The Psychology of Child Education: Nurturing Future Generations
5. Ethical Enlightenment: A Modern Guide to Living with Integrity
6. Voices of Empowerment: Stories of Women Rising Against Odds
7. Social Psychology in Everyday Life: Understanding Human Connections
8. The Essence of Motivational Speaking: Inspiring Change in Others
9. Balancing Acts: Women, Work, and the Will to Lead
10. Guiding with Grace: Raising Children with Compassion and Awareness
11. The Power of Positive Aging: Embracing Life After Fifty
12. Building Resilient Communities: Social Work in Action
13. The Ethical Educator: Principles for Teaching and Learning
14. From Insight to Impact: Social Psychology for a Better World
15. The Ethics of Empathy: A Guide to Ethical Living
16. The Science of Empowering the Self: Navigating Life's Challenges with Psychological Wisdom
17. The Mindful Conscious Leader: Meditation Techniques for Modern Management
18. Pioneering Spirit: Women's Pathways to Leadership and Empowerment
19. Feeling to Healing: The Role of Emotional Intelligence in Child Development
20. Transformative Talks and Words of Inspiration: Insights into Motivational Oratory

21. Green Ethics: A Path to Sustainable Living
22. Spiritual Integrity: Navigating Life with Moral Compassion
23. Clean Living, Clean Society: The Ethics of Cleanliness
24. Patriotic Spirits: Building a Nation on Positive Attitudes
25. Innovative Integrity & Vibrant Visions: The Ethical and Entrepreneurial Spirit of Gujarat
26. Youthful Visions, Endless Possibilities: Inspiring Ethics and Motivation in Children
27. Living Your Legacy: How to Motivate Others by Living Your Values
28. Secret of Healing Conversations: Ethical Practices in Counselling and Therapy
29. Creative Kindness: Crafting a Life of Compassion and Creativity
30. The Power of Appreciation: How Gratitude Can Transform Your Relationships
31. Bhagavad-Gita: Messages
32. Science of Art: The New Frontier of Fashion Modernism
33. Vivekananda's Virtues: A Blueprint for Modern Living
34. Empower Her: Navigating the Path to Women's Entrepreneurship
35. The Boundless Classroom: Innovations in Global Education
36. The Language of Leadership: Communicating with Authenticity and Impact
37. The Warrior's Mantra: Deciphering the Hanuman Chalisa
38. Echoes of Empathy: Transformative Stories of Social Service
39. Artful Living: Cultivating Creativity in Your Daily Routine
40. Finding Your Why: Discovering Your Passions and Charting Your Course
41. The Role of Social Media in Shaping Self-Esteem and Interpersonal Relationships among Adolescents
42. Karma's Tapestry: Weaving a Life of Selfless Service
43. Altruistic Alchemy: Transforming Lives Through Giving
44. The Blueprint of Pro-Activeness and Productivity: Crafting Habits for Success
45. The Simplicity with Grounded Wisdom: Embracing Authenticity

Bhajan

101. Pilgrimage of the Soul: Spiritual Journeys in India

❦❦❦

Contact

Dr. Minakshi Bansal
Social Activist
Ahmedabad, Gujarat, Bharat
minakshiindiag20@yahoo.com

ᗐᗐᗐ

|| LOKAHA SAMASTHAHA SUKHINO BHAVANTU ||